THE WHOLE THING

Michael Foley

The Whole Thing
published in the United Kingdom in 2023
by Mica Press

c/o Leslie Bell
47 Belle Vue Road, Wivenhoe, Colchester, Essex CO7 9LD
www.micapress.co.uk | books@micapress.co.uk

ISBN 978-1-869848-32-3
© Michael Foley 2023

For Martina

Again a day as, undiminished and unwearied by its journey
from the sun, ardent light slips with ease around
the curtains fully drawn to radiate over the ceiling in spokes
and emblazon the wall with a strip of bright gold,
and the great tree just outside the window, though rooted,
and lacking a breeze to inspire it, is once more excited.
In the shock waves that emanate still from creation
the branches are trembling, the leaves are astir,
and now is heard a jubilant clarion, herald of morning,
a trumpet blast to summon forth from slumber the soul,
complementing aurally the rays on the ceiling –
a succinct but wholly distinctive fart from Ray next door.

There is no obligation to rise – and with the beloved
still away I can spread in a star shape to revel in bed space.
This just after waking is the inspiration time. Dreams exercise
the mind with random associating, making work those
lazy synapses, training them, so that, when consciousness returns,
new and unlikely but thrilling connections spark and hum.
And here comes today's new idea (in fact very old) –
that *everything* is related and *everything* is process.
There is nothing substantial (no ultimate stuff),
nothing conclusive or final (no endstates), nothing immutable
(never a fixity), nothing reducible (no independent parts),
nothing predictable (never necessity), nothing repeatable
(never a same), and no absolute or ideal (no beyond).
There is only the unity in process of everything connected to
everything, everything changed by and changing everything.
And the whole thing is therefore to be a whole thing
that is wholly immersed in the greater whole thing.

So give yourself. Strip naked. Step in. Get under
the glittering sunflower and gasp once again at
cold impact on sweating soiled shivering bare flesh.
This is reality. This is the cold truth. Bear it …
Wear it. Don with pride the flashing silver cloak
of flow that clothes the Gods, that *is* the Gods.
Be only flow to be divine. It is all a flowing,
all a flow. Not a thing permanent. Not a thing solid.
The bare creature also a creation of flow,
a mere vortex of energy flowing through.

A conduit of divinity. God is flow. Raise open
palms in acceptance and gratitude, lift up the face
for a vehement, pointillist head massage
that brings an alert trance, a rigorous associating
reverie as notions incompatible find forbidden love
and breed. It is all flowing oneness, though a unity
of opposites, relaxant and stimulant, a surrender to
flow that yet stands up to flow, immerses to transcend,
goes deep to get high and conforms to transgress.
To the song of the sunflower my tuneless croak.
To the silver shower my yellow piss. I am one
with the oneness, everything and its opposite,
God and a nobody, powerless but monarch of all
I survey. Enough revelation for one day. A towel
to cover the creature that can't tolerate long exposure
but must dress again for its role as a person of substance,
departing the vortex that swirls round the plughole,
convinced it will flourish for ever but going abruptly
down the drain with a gurgle of disbelief, rage and despair.

Aflow in the process, at one with the oneness
I gladly partake of the wealth of this promised land
flowing with pasteurised semi-skimmed milk and organic honey
of forest bees. For the first of my daily five pieces of fruit,
I snap from a bunch a long banana, fat and firm, its brown stalk
the prow of a Polynesian war canoe painted yellow
for a festival and conveying in tribute to a king
fruit to slice in his luxury muesli. Yellow is the colour
of happiness so I bare yellow teeth in a grateful grin.

And here is the first sacrament of the day. 'Body and blood
of Christ,' I intone, to transubstantiate mint tea and multigrain toast
and make this day a quest for the hidden quotidian,
the eternal diurnal, not its macro desires and frustrations
but its micro adventures and satisfactions, its sacraments
and rituals from matins to vespers, their utensils and vessels,
and the multiple rewards of unitasking, the practice, subversive
and spiritual, of doing, alone and in silence, one thing at a time.
Today there is time. For the Lord hath anointed me
with the balm of retirement. I toil not and neither do I spin
mission statements nor project proposals and neither go in

with dissemblers and sit with vain persons in meetings
but here in my own home commune with my heart
in my own swivel chair and be still. Now in
the cool serenity of morning everything is possible.
There is time ... whole, uncalibrated. This is about time.

Intending to take my time, I commence with the writing
preparation rite - sharpening three pencils one by one, carefully,
in an old sharpener, full of old shavings but still releasing
fragrance when I thrust in the soiled, blunted head and give
the body a twist, which the blade at first delightfully resists ...
but then dull grey surface skin springs off like apple peel over a knife
to release a fresh wood scent, reveal zesty brightness
beneath and a surgical point that can prick and pierce,
although this is no longer the point because neither
disgust nor contempt but praise alone renews the soul.
So *give praise and take heart*, I say once again as I drive the old head
deeper in and impart to the old wood and lead a sharp twist.
Then I place the last pencil point-up in a jar and incant
the propitiatory morning prayer: God, Goddess, Ground of Being,
Demiurge, World Spirit, Shiva, Tao, Beloved, whatever the name,
you who invest with such richness and mystery cosmos and earth,
possess me, inspire me, endow me and fire me.

> Bestow on me now a late break.
> I'm sixty-nine for fuck's sake
>
> But only just seeing how strange it all is.
> I want to make a whole song and dance about this.
>
> So raise up my passionate benison
> To the falsetto heights of Roy Orbison,
>
> Grace my shamanic dance
> With Fred Astaire elegance.
>
> Let's make *The Whole Thing*
> Shamble, soar, sing and swing.

But to celebrate the small is no small undertaking. Since everything is
connected to everything else and possesses a history conditioned by and
conditioning everything else, in order to understand anything it is necessary not

just to understand everything but also the history of everything, including one's own unique, complex and constantly unfolding history.

'All things are interwoven with one another,' said Aurelius. 'Everything is linked and works together giving form to the one universe.'

So, to explain the minutiae of a day requires the chronicle of a life, which in turn requires the history of the universe to date.

Therefore, to try to grasp everything, let mingle high and low, micro and macro, far and near, east and west, present and past, sub-atomic and supra-galactic, mythic and mundane, divine and profane, the historical sweep and the daily creep, the tales of a fleeting speck of dust and the enduring immensity in which it floats, the absurd and sublime.

And let mingle disciplines, genres and specialisms. Come at it every way possible – it takes a shitload of epistemological diversity to get any kind of grip on ontological unity. Many and winding are the ways to the One.

With a telescope at one eye and a microscope at the other, in the left hand Chuang Tzu and in the right hand a physics book, the left brain fretfully enquiring if this is science or a fairy tale, philosophy or religion, history or mythology, reverence or blasphemy, fiction or naked truth, poetry or prose, and the freely-associating right brain replying that *The Whole Thing* is all these and much more, plus jokes.

So raise and fire the starting gun for the big bang
that triggers the whole thing. We're off!
Let my universe develop from the point of a pencil,
as did the real one, the cosmologists say, from an even more
microscopic point, but becoming immediately a maelstrom,
raging already with the duelling dualities, the vying opposites,
matter and antimatter attempting to annihilate each other
and gravity trying to pull together what energy tries to drive apart.

Now fast forward billions of years – and the same opposition
is still playing out … in a Northern Irish living room
as parents attempt to impose their gravity on a young boy
exploding with energy, the father crying, 'easy … go *easy*',
and the mother, 'Would ye give over acting the maggot'
(or 'the tin man', 'the eejit', 'the monkey', 'the goat'),
the boy thinking, 'No, I most certainly won't'
and, like Phaethon hurling the Chariot of the Gods across the skies,
furiously pedalling his tricycle right to the end of the street.

Or defying gravity in the high places, making leaps of faith
from crag to crag of Father Hegarty's Rock, while the fearful mother
implores him, 'In the *name of God* would ye come down outa that',
and when he refuses, cries in peevishness, 'Well don't expect *me*
to go runnin' to the Infirmary when ye break your neck.'
And though he can never score goals or even keep goal,
accurately throw stones, drink a bottle of school milk in one go,
spit a green gob without moving his lips or do Tarzan's yell,
he has learned to defy gravity by going along with it,
'drop', as they put it, the Lucky Lane wall, hanging from the top
of the wall, feet in toeholds, gauging the distance,
then letting go and kicking out into the heady rush of free fall,
before landing delicately on his feet like a cat.

So into the void the exultant dust soared, to cavort,
gambol, dance, laugh and sing. Dust is the master of the universe.
For only the dust is immortal. Only the dust is invincible.
Only the dust is a protean shape shifter. Only the dust
knows no boundaries. Only the dust will abide.
Only the dust can lie low or fly high, seep, sift, drift
or float, defy gravity in lightness or exert crushing weight,
in a storming host obliterate or, grain by insidious grain, infiltrate.

Yet the desperate mother, like a priest casting out evil spirits,
with a special bat beats dust from carpets hung out on the line,
with a cloth wipes it off polished tables and shelves
and pursues it into corners with a screaming machine,
crying, 'Lift up your feet would ye lift up your feet outa that,'
to the scowling boy trying to watch *Wagon Train*.
And the dust of course is happy to seem to submit, to have such
raging fools to outwit. Wasn't it for pleasures like this it made life?
Hey, let's have something that moves by itself … and can
reproduce, evolve and learn. A brute that can think
and has therefore more shite in its head than its bowels.
Who knows what might happen then? *What larks, Pip!*
No, this creature is too much at home in the garden.
Let a shaman cut nicks on a bone to mark the phases
of the moon and believe he has mastered time
by measuring when it is time that has mastered him.
Now eternity dies, time is born, God retreats up to heaven,
the creature is cast from the garden and falls into time,

fated to yearn to understand but never know what it is, what it wants,
what it does, though, aware now of death, always see where it goes.

Therefore into the perilous world the quest heroes go forth –
and up into attic rooms, pondering, scribbling, seekers of truth,
and the smirking dust silently sifts in the truth-seeking homes
and rises in clouds from the quest hero's roads. First out
is Gilgamesh, king of earliest city Uruk, surpassing all kings
in his beauty and wealth, but consumed by a constant fear of death,
which waits for him always out on the roads, on the farthermost seas
and in the innermost chambers of his turbulent heart.
Outwards or inwards, wherever he turns he is confronted by death.
He must set out in search of the plant of immortality.
So he penetrates to the heart of the forest, slays Humbaba
the terrible monster, and rejects the advances of the beautiful Ishtar,
the Goddess whose loins burn with fire at his splendour:
'Be mine and your goats will bear triplets, your donkeys
will outrun the chariot horses. Come to me, Gilgamesh.
I will honour your beauty with tribute. I will rub you
with rich oils and suck your sweet rod.'

But he turns away and journeys on to the edge of the world,
outruns the very sun, sails even over the Waters of Death
and dives through the Great Deep to bring back the priceless plant
… only to fall asleep and have it stolen by a snake.
'So all my hardships have been for nothing. Was it for this
that my hands have laboured, for this I gave my heart's blood,
wandered the world, scaled the treacherous mountains, crossed deserts,
sailed oceans, while rarely has gentle sleep softened my brow?'

Also leaving home to seek the elixir of life, the boy goes to *The Palace*,
and on a balding velvet seat in the sumptuous wet-dog-smelling dim,
enduring the torture of an overfull bladder so as not to miss even one
radiant scene, he follows, enraptured, his first mentor, master, his first
fearless quest hero, golden-haired, buckskin-clad Shane (Alan Ladd).
Shane settles down with a family, or tries to, but not for the seeker
the life of such people (Jean Arthur, Van Heflin and Brandon de Wilde
the young son). When he slays the sneering monster (Jack Palance)
and rides away into the night, alone, noble, wounded, unbroken, still golden,
the boy lingers on, deaf to up-slamming seats and the coarse shouts

of oafs, and cries in his grieving heart with Brandon de Wilde,
abandoned now with boring dependable parents, the last echoing cry
in the stricken night, 'I love you, Shane. *Shane! Shane! Come back!*'

But the boy's mother, giving her all to the struggle with dust,
believes now that her son is a fool. For he values not the dustless home,
nor yet the gravity of attaining a better station in life.
He loves not to revere the august but to laugh with the dust.
Madness and folly in his heart, he goes every Saturday to the library
in Brooke Park and exultantly carries six heavy books back.

What is he seeking? Where should he look? Blindly, furiously,
stubbornly, he seeks the divine energy of the shaman in Biggles books.
Certain of being part royal and part divine, it comes to him
that he must be a changeling, the son of a Goddess and a Philosopher King.
It is certainly not his ineluctable destiny to be the timorous son of this
timorous pair, father asleep in his armchair, mother brooding by the fire.
As *his* mouth falls more slackly open, the drawstrings of *her* mouth
pull more tightly closed. And now a snore draws forth a sneer.

So - how to escape without leaving? How to rebel without
breaking the rules? How to exult without showing emotion?
Books, books, books … occult elixir … secret wings.
He belongs not with peers but with Alice and the sibling four,
those for whom earth - or a wardrobe door - opens up
onto a hidden world. Exile yourself in your secret heart
and repeat to the deep-pile carpet and rugs, the three-piece
velvet suite and the long velvet curtains that shut out
the light: *my mother the Goddess, my father the King.*

High above the noisome pestilence of the toughs on the street,
to an attic room next to the stars he retreats, to solve problems
of gravity and energy with the iron laws of Newton's mechanics,
unaware that these are fifty years out of date. In strict accordance
with the laws, pulley systems make weights rise and fall,
heavy pendulums swing to and fro, spheres collide and diverge
on computable trajectories, and, in equally orderly, linear motion,
masses descend inclined, friction-free planes. Everything works
out as logic prescribes. To know exactly what will happen,

list the variables, choose the equations, substitute values and solve.
The whole thing is determined by timeless laws.
It can all be predicted, precisely computed. Maths is the absolute,
outside of time. Maths is pure, eternal, omniscient ... divine.
Whereas life is disgustingly runny, unclean -
the viscid mucous creeping from the nostrils of the low.

This is the age of solidity, for people of substance abhorring process
- the authoritarian stabilitarian. No change because we forbid change,
they boom, moving like Newton's planetary bodies, solemnly,
sedately and magisterially, on orbits precisely predetermined,
through a void as invisible, mute and submissive
as the country maid from Killybegs in the next attic room.
Theirs is a decorous universe with no exploding supernovae,
hidden dark matter or dark energy, a mechanical universe
whose prehistoric megalith is the grandfather clock in the silent hall.
Its ponderous pendulum swings no more, for its function
is not to tell time but declare that here time has agreed to stand still.
The role of this clock is to proclaim timeless rule - to enforce,
preside ... grandly and darkly to loom, as, far again above
the brooding hall and attic room, the delinquent void ripples
and seethes and writhes, exploding for kicks a senile star.

And on Halloween when the dark energy visits the earth
the boy puts lit bangers in jam jars to blow them apart,
or tosses them through the letter boxes on the good end of the street
to alarm those dim halls and their tomb-guardian clocks.
Be it known that in the first days of his omnipotence he will return
to his school - but in the cab of a crane with a wrecking ball,
and he will have Father O'Flaherty publicly strung up and, by each
in turn of the boys he hurt, flogged with his own leather strap,
and he will demonstrate his mastery of Newtonian gravity
by dropping the grandfather clock from the attic on top of
the mocking gang in the street and especially the leader
who sneered, in disgust and contempt, 'You're a *worm*'.

At the back of his secret drawer lies his treasure, neatly wrapped
in waxed paper, his talisman, totem, far surpassing in aura
the Swiss knife, brass compass, American dollar and Chilean stamps
- the razor blade stolen from his father. At night he opens

12

the paper and reverently takes out the blade, exhilaratingly dangerous
even to handle, the most menacing thing in a sheltered world,
the thinnest thing in a fat world … insanely thin, like Jack Palance
in *Shane*, glinting with cool, sadistic malice, an efficient killer
with a shark's grin (its indented slit like a shark mouth and teeth)
or Jack's mirthless wolf grin. This blade refuses all practical chores,
such as sharpening pencils, bending away in amused disdain,
wanting only to kill or wound deeply, slice swiftly
and cleanly through flesh to a vein.

But enough of this ancient malevolence. Now my old heart wishes
only to praise. My stiff limbs want only to join in the dance.
My cracked voice wants only to rise up in song.

      So awake, harp and psaltery,
      For fervent idolatry

      Of every worldly thing that has been
      Sniffed, tasted, touched, heard or seen,

      Then recreated in loving mimesis
      Or forensically taken to pieces.

      Unite, senses and brain,
      To present *and* explain.

Therefore I swiftly spin my Ergo Mesh Executive Swivel Chair
(with breathable seat pad and multi-adjustable lumbar function)
and roll it across to the window, the better once again to see
le vierge, le vivace et le bel aujourd'hui. Fairer by far than the courts
of the Pharaoh is the railway track bordered by tangled embankments,
with dead brambles, overturned shopping carts, rotting
FOR SALE boards and the back wall of Sidings Community Centre,
defiled on three levels by hoardings, graffiti and arsonists'
scorch marks, but still, unassailably, Mont Sainte-Victoire.

Once more the mystery of dark human consciousness
in the even greater mystery of the radiant world.
Life is the momentary contact of two deep unknowns

– a bright sky briefly shining on the surface of a well.

Long, long, I sit and dwell. Long, long, I gaze and muse.
It is all, simultaneously, more familiar and more strange.
The more known the deeper the mystery. Always it comes
to this: seat, window, world, and a reverie of bewilderment
at that baffling unity in process, a life – how the mystery
of being young becomes, imperceptibly, the even more
perplexing mystery of having grown old. Be still now,
counsels the ageing heart. But there is no now and nothing
is still. By the rusty tracks that lead to the horizon,
the triumphalist leaves of the Japanese knotweed, barbarian
conqueror, sway like the standards of an army advancing,
as a ripple traverses the unsubdued grasses, moving swiftly
above the earth with the nonchalant, ethereal grace of a dancer.
There is even a murmur of running water, the natural music
of oneness and flow. Is this the Heraclitus River that no one
steps in twice? No, it's Ray's water feature next door.
There the mouth of a Roman God pours loudly into
a dark pool where golden fish inscrutably poise and point.
Here a glistening filigree links up the drainpipe
and window frame and an intricate, formerly invisible,
spider web comes in view, trembling but holding.
Cease from your weaving and the pattern appears.

Now a smattering of little birds alight on the garden wall
and desperately peck at the bare brick. Why?
And who do I think I am? Where, when and what
is my only life? How did I get to be sixty-nine?

No reply. The response time is bad today. Must be the server.
No, here's a message arriving the old way, soon to be obsolete
and heard no more, the thrilling thump on the hall floor.
It's a letter from Raymond McCandless to tell me
that one of the street toughs has died, and including
the local paper with the death notice marked. I experience
a sudden stab of loss … oh not for the dead brute
(Raymond was always a bit soft) but because of the new,
unfamiliar names that replace the old cinemas, dancehalls
and bars. All the sacred sites of my youth have been

wiped out without even *notifying*, much less *consulting*, me.
Without even any *awareness* of me. Reduced to dust
even the temples and palaces. Even *The Palace* on
Shipquay Street where I first was enraptured by *Shane*.

All returned to the dust. But elsewhere in this paper
hides the real message, potent, stinging, revelatory:
On Quiz Night in the Telstar's refurbished back lounge
The Fly Men's long winning run came to an end
when top honours went to debut team The Four Babes
- Lily Barr, Rosaleen Hegarty, Monica Sheeran and Deirdre McDaid.
Luminiferous names blazing fiercely as quasars down darkening years.
So many billions of years have gone by, not to mention
over sixty-nine of mine. Lord, it must be coffee time.

To the lazy eye all are alike but in fact no two coffee beans
are identical. Each has the cut-in-half-ovoid shape,
but is morphically distinct, with unique striation patterns
on the ovoid face and a singular trench running through
the flat side. Often this trench has a curl or turns up at one end,
creating a twisted-grin effect. But *these* beans would never make
a smiley face. These are French, roasted expressly for bitterness.
For we need to inoculate with doses of bitterness.
Believing that life is sweet is what makes it sour.
Neither would this bean flaunt or preen. It knows
that it's vulgar to glitter but acceptable ... even sophisticated
... to *gleam*. A twisted grin and dark gleam.
The size and shape of a tiny beetle but avoiding
by means of its colour entomological distaste.
There is something reassuring in a rich dark brown, the colour
of tradition with character, mahogany furniture and old leather,
which also both gleam. Good to roll between finger and thumb,
the odd shape rejecting any obvious easy turn. And hard.
It won't crumble ... crushable only by hammer or grinder.
Which of course will be its fate - but not yet.
Today both bean and drinker will enjoy a rare treat,
the opening of a large new packet of beans.
In goes the hand, plunging deep and becoming immersed
completely in beans, which seem to gambol and cavort,
around, through and over the fingers. Listen now
- a broad river of beans is pouring into the tin,

the percussion music deepening as the tin fills
and the centre of gravity of the packet shifts to provide,
as it empties, a feeling of buoyancy, even liftoff.
Shed the load, relish the lightness, get high and fly.
High already – and the rocket blast of caffeine still to come.

In the solemn sacrament of morning I place in the grinder
two full scoops of beans, time the grind so the coffee, like writing,
is neither too coarse nor too fine, and transfer it carefully
to the holder, trying not to spill even one precious grain.
Then I take up the tamper, a beautiful object to handle
with two metal discs on each side of a rod, the larger disc
snug in the palm as the smaller disc shepherds the grains
on the edge of the holder back into the centre for
the tamping that provides the satisfaction of compression
(again analogous to writing), a tighter, firmer
and neater unity with a pleasingly uniform face.
This is such a pleasure that I usually tamp down twice,
each time as scrupulously as I tamp down my ego
(never lose your tamper, the Masters repeat).
After inspection for stray grains I slot the holder
into the stalwart arm, engage the arm in the machine
and pull it tight, enjoying stiff resistance. Then I wait
in reverence with bowed head – for this is the consecration,
when the grains are transubstantiated into the ichor of God,
which, topped like the bitter black sea waves with foam,
is solemnly delivered to the sacred vessel,
my dodecahedronal, bottle-green cup rimmed with gold.

The aroma of brewing coffee was surely the fragrance
of the morning in heaven when God had His dream
of creating the world, and a sip of black arabica,
with the bitterness of chlorogenic acids but an aftertaste
of chocolate, gave Him a vision of bitter-sweet, a world unfolding
in infinite mystery and a finite creature to marvel and grieve.
So now coffee blesses all the ordinary things of this world
– cup, pencil, desk, screen and keyboard, across the track,
the wall with the six-foot signature of graffiti artist, TOX 1,
then the railway line litter and weeds, and on this side
Ray's satellite dish with a pigeon on top, and the urgent flap
of the plastic sheet on the loft conversion up the street.

Solemnly I grip, sniff, sip, observe, listen … ponder.
Then as solemnly cleanse the sacred vessels, scoop and tamper.
Ah nobler by far than to be yet another chronicler of heroes
and kings, is to serve as the amanuensis of common unregarded things,
to banish the snobbery of organic chauvinism and acknowledge
the rights of our maker, matter, on the surface inert but wild at heart,
playing dead to hide its bizarre inner life, an exemplary
non-attention-seeker. Emulate matter - appear silent, still and opaque,
an enigma, but pullulate and churn with secret, sovereign energy,
and appreciate matter's true value, not financial, instrumental
or ornamental, but *transcendental*, the remote and inscrutable
entelechy of *stuff*. Learn to attend to the teaching of the inanimate,
things in their rapt meditation repeating that silence is
the eloquent speech, and stillness the concentrated energy, of God.

Therefore I wash my cereal bowl and dirty spoon
as reverently as the feet of Christ the Lord.
For the spoon is a mystic that cradles the light it so
ardently hoards in a curved, compressed, inverted world,
and, after the staff, the bowl is the only accessory of
the humble seeker going forth, demanding to be lifted carefully
with hands turned up and open in the gesture of blessings
accepted or given. Life is a quest, they repeat, not a feast.
We are meant not to gorge but to ponder and seek.

Raymond McCandless, tell me how, when at dusk
the light began to fade on the raucous, belligerent street,
we were both entranced and silent, apart from the toughs,
as they screamed at intruders from other streets or caught
and tortured stray cats. Recall to me cheevies, chasing girls
- for the first time the mystery incarnate, through the dim night
real nymphs with wild rapturous cries. There goes the boy I was,
gladly ensorcelled, following as Cathy O'Kane runs before,
darting and swerving, a young doe, veering off then into
Duffy's garden and settling delicately on the grass,
carefully arranging her spread dress. At the garden gate
he stops dead, transfixed for the first time by the terror
of beauty, the spell of the Goddess, as a brazen tough,
the one who has called him a worm, roughly shoves past
and falls on the girl with a yell.

Raymond, Raymond, my old friend, where are the portals,
where is the path, and what the wild steps of the transporting dance?
No, Raymond, alas, you were always a bit on the slow side,
always the cautious one, scarcely a shaman, never tempted
to go forth impulsively, like Jason, whose insouciant progress
we followed laboriously in Father McGlinchey's classics class.

From his home in Iolcos, Jason, son of the exiled king Aeson,
sails away into the unknown, in search of the Golden Fleece
that endows, enables and transforms, navigating through
the sharp rocks of the Symplegades, to the kingdom of Aietes,
where he blithely accepts the king's impossible challenges
– tame the bulls with horns of bronze and breath of flame,
make them plough a stony field, sow it with dragon's teeth,
and then kill the armed men who spring up from this seed.
Medea, the king's young daughter, stirred by the assurance
and grace of Jason, puts to work her skill as a sorceress
by offering Jason superhuman invulnerability and strength,
on condition only that after his triumph he take her for wife.
Empowered by Medea's enchantments and potions,
Jason, intoxicated, fearless, wearing no armour
but arrogant confidence, vanquishes bulls and armed men,
runs to the oak grove of Ares, slays the malevolent
guarding dragon and rips from the oak tree the Golden Fleece.

In Iolcos Medea, with magic herbs and rituals, rejuvenates Aeson,
who is brought back from exile and crowned king once more,
and with cruel enchantments destroys Aeson's rivals.
But the people rise against Medea and drive her and Jason
into exile, where Jason abandons Medea and takes as his new wife
the young princess Creusa. The wedding presents from Medea
– a poisoned robe and a palace fire that burns to death Creusa.
Then Medea summons Jason, slays before his eyes their children
and departs forever from the earth in a chariot drawn by two dragons.
The once fearless Jason, become old and broken, wanders
the seashore and lingers by the rotting hulk of his great ship, the Argo,
which bore him off into the perilous unknown and now,
also exhausted and broken, collapses on top of, and kills, the quest hero.

To wear only the armour of arrogant ease and bear no shield

but radiance and no blade but grace! Raymond, we were pale,
blotchy, scourgey and snottery - marred, blemished, timorous -
and the golden fleece was the olive skin of Cathy O'Kane,
a legendary princess, daughter of the pharmacist Eugene O'Kane,
far out of reach in the very best part of the good end of the street.
Youth, Raymond, youth ... that violent maelstrom of rage,
desire, hatred, despair and shame. Coveting everything, knowing
nothing ... blundering, messing, deeply unprepossessing.
Never so much craved, so little achieved.

Wherewithal shall a young man cleanse his way? With the purity
and chastity of higher mathematics, wise and beautiful equations
that balance the world like the harmony of Justice balancing scales.
The ultimate rational is mystical. God is the Infinite Book
of Theorems defining the Oneness, and out of these theorems
flows linear logic that leads in an orderly, inexorable chain of
A implying B and B implying C to the inevitable answer ... QED.
It can all be explained by the timeless proofs that preside
in mathematical heaven far from the timebound toiling world.
To be a magus of science - physics or chemistry ...
but never biology. Everything animate is messy, smelly, sticky,
slimy, crusty, oozing and seeping, dripping and weeping,
infiltrating, contaminating, its fluids and odours and slimy
integuments disgustingly unclean and treacherous, slipping through
the groping fingers and running rings round the linear brain,
always problematical and, worse, unmathematical, breeding
in mud and swamp and ocean far from the pure equations
of heaven. Mathematical biology - a joke oxymoron.

But to follow the equations and penetrate the heart of inanimate matter,
or to fly to the edge of the universe, in the thrilling embrace
of the winged God Hypothesis! Forget swords and dragons
and beautiful maidens. The grail is a verifiable Theory of Everything.
To rip off the mask of the Inscrutable Oneness and bare to all the mind
of God. But oh Lord, the tedious, trivial experiments. The Bunsen
burners, flasks and beakers. The calibrated pipettes, scales and meters.

The great discovery comes in Lecture Theatre 3, but long after dark,
black-out blinds all down, the right time for the Film Club to show,
to a few troubled seekers here and there on hard benches,

an old grainy black-and-white based on an old play,
The Long Day's Journey Into Night … about a claustrophobic family
with a young son who quotes mad but stirring French poetry.
Who is this Eugene O'Neill, with the name of a jovial
hometown burgher but such an enthrallingly black tale to tell?
And who this exemplary lunatic Baudelaire whose advice
is to keep intoxication alive? Could the Baudelaire strategy be right …
spend the day reading mad dogs' shite and the night drinking wine?
And who is Jason Robards Jnr, so intensely the alcoholic,
ruined older brother, wanting his sibling to do well but also,
in one dark scene, to fail? This brother exists in two places at once …
Like an elementary particle. The human heart must be as strange
as the atom. A and Not A can be both true at once.

Oh but the tedium of days in the lab. 'To be a practical person
has always seemed especially horrible,' says Baudelaire.
'Enthusiasm for anything other than abstraction is a sign
of weakness and disease'. The quest hero values his mind
not his hands. Apparatus defeats him. No lab work completed,
yet reports to submit. But it has come to pass that he has
come to pass … Make the mind justify its primacy and *think*.
Experimental blunders are now all the rage. Geniuses love things
to go wrong. Disaster is what makes them think and learn.
So, alone in another attic room, he invents failed experiments
so touchingly plausible he could weep real tears for his fake mistakes.
Then pretends to investigate each mistake … and, behold, every
cul-de-sac is a portal of truth. It's the long night's journey into day,
when a radiant dawn reveals the way – to invent a truth *truer than fact*.

Now begins the pure life of the garret, far from venality and close
to eternity, the visionary ecstatic in the vatic attic. To be free
and alone, in autonomous majesty, protecting the unsullied essence
of soul, as singular and inscrutable as a prime number,
avid and mordant, high above the contaminating clutch
of the world. 'Glory is always to remain *one*', says Baudelaire.
Everything noble is born in an upper room. Poetry and philosophy
are always in upper rooms. On the top floor of a bookshop he steals
Penguin Classics. The fearless despisers – Baudelaire and Flaubert,
Nietzsche and Schopenhauer, with exhilarating contempt
for almost everything, but especially religion, politics, journalism,
commerce and the vulgar pleasures of the common herd,

despisers of democracy, employment and marriage – the rule
of the mob, the domain of the bully, the trap of the family.
'Life,' explains Flaubert, 'is like a nauseating kitchen smell
that pours through a ventilator. You don't have to eat
what they're cooking to know it will make you throw up.'

Reveal none of this to the common herd, the cynical nihilists.
P is for poetry and philosophy but also for poser and phoney.
The jackals would love to leer, drag down and lacerate.
In secret, on high in the garret, imbibe P elixirs in solitary rapture.
'I have built myself a tower,' declared Flaubert proudly,
'and now let the waves of shit beat at its base.'
Nietzsche higher again: 'Let us live far above
like the strong winds, neighbours of eagles, the snow and the sun.'

The cool of the high and the high of the cool. The exhilarating
freedom of upper air, unassailable power of the view from on high,
looking down without emotion on the crawlers in the mire.
I'd have made a great sniper … if I hadn't ruined my eyes reading.

Remembering now the divine ebriety of upper rooms, I spin and rock
my swivel chair. My Ergo's my Argo. I sail it once more to the window
and find it has rained hard. The patio flags are wet and dark.
The flame-of-the-forest leaves shine and turn, and the arc of
the clothesline, threaded with brilliant beads, asway in a light breeze,
is surely the necklace on the breast of the Goddess.

But O Goddess, here go the knights of King Arthur, clanging
in full armour, brandishing swords and escutcheoned shields,
thundering on snorting steeds. *Ride you then so hotly on a quest so holy?*
Bold indeed is the answer, *Stay us not.* For the souls of these knights
have been set on fire by a burning vision of the Holy Grail
in Arthur's Hall and they believe that if a man could but touch
the Grail he would be healed at once of ills and pain.
Go forth, this shining vision urged, defeat the foes, evade the lures,
and be crowned King far in the spiritual city. Whereupon all
foreswore all vainglories and joys, the revelries of halls
that heat the blood and the rivalries of jousts that win hearts of the fair.
'Ye follow a wandering fire,' Arthur warns, 'that would lead you and lose

you in desert and quagmire.' But the knights heed him not and swear a vow
to ride a twelvemonth and a day through pagan realms to seek the Grail.

On they ride, to battle with heathen hordes, cross high seas
driving like cataracts, wander in a wilderness of sand and thorns,
endure lightnings, furnace heats, dust storms like rivers clouding heaven,
then a black swamp blanched by the bones of men, and a hill
encircled by permanent fire. On yet, on, Sir Bors de Ganis, Galahad,
son of Launcelot, and Percevale le Gallois. Comes Sir Bors to
an high tower where a lady, young, lusty and fair, receives him
with great joy and makes him to sit and, on roasted meats
and many dainties, bids him sup and drink with her.
And maidens lead Percevale to a magnificent castle whose Lady
is the one who made in youth his heart leap, her husband now dead
and his wealth hers, but her longing and will all to Percevale
as of old, so that every day she sets a banquet richer than before
and every day in his heart fades the quest for the Grail.

Alone, where a thousand piers and bridges meet a great sea,
Galahad leaps from pier to pier, and quickly, as he crosses,
each behind is consumed in fire, till into a boat on the great sea
he leaps, and above him for a moment shines in fire the Holy Grail.
Then seen upon this earth no more are Galahad and Holy Grail.

Now the young Irish quest hero harks to the call. The time for
the crossing of the threshold is at hand. But where are the wise ones,
the masters? The kind ones, the mentors? The wild ones, the shamans?

To the court of King James, the Sun King of the North, improbably
based in Portrush, the Babylon, Gomorrah and Las Vegas
of the North, where, surrounded by courtiers, a mighty queen,
many bold children and ladies in waiting, to a rapturous chorus,
King James sings The Great Yes to Truth, Love and Life …
his Palace a ramshackle rundown old house that defiantly acknowledges
the primacy of dust. Accept and rejoice in decay, it insists,
decay was the first and best abstract expressionist, blending
together dirt, stains, mould and rust. And that the meaning
of life is dissolution is also the message in the Harbour Bar,
with whiskey on whiskey consumed through the night.

The Irish quest hero's first test is the challenge of whiskey.
Mentor or monster? The potion of shamans or the poison of demons?

Exhausted by drink and the spitefulness of courtiers, the hero walks out
of the Harbour Bar and into the night, where he launches his rank steaming
jet at what seem the eternally cold stars and void. For youth the universe
is fixed, the immutable scenery for the imminent drama, youth's trajectory
of fire - space, time, the heavens and even the human world merely a grey
unchanging grid. Let the fiery progress of youth begin! *Fiat Lux*!
Only years reveal the whole thing as a roiling, rolling, swirling,
unfurling, mutating, creating, densely interconnected and unified flux.

Born from the dust, just like us, are the stars that seem coldly eternal
                    And unto dust they shall return
                    But not before they pulse and burn,
Contract, expand, collide, explode in supernovae, as fierily mental
                    As cauldron minds of adolescents,
                    In a fury that forges new elements.

And they form symbiotic pair relationships for reasons not understood,
                    Take from and dance with each other,
                    Frequently even devour each other,
And just as frequently get divorced and fly far apart through the void,
                    Their binary evolution as complex,
                    Necessary and mysterious as sex.

But no ... never cold, still, eternal ... it's all fiery, mortal endeavour
                    Fighting deadly gravity with energy
                    And fiercely resisting degeneracy
By keeping their weight down. The light stars live almost forever
                    But all die as white dwarfs, black holes.
                    Lord have mercy on their burning souls.

The stars that appear so fastidiously remote, so timelessly pale and cold,
are in reality industrial furnaces, cosmic foundries forging
heavy elements, the raw material of matter and organisms, stuff and us.
Our planet and all that is on it was made out of stardust.
So everything on earth is unearthly, and the void that seems so still,
inert and empty is a muscle-flexing, effervescing field of energy.

King Jimmy's path of excess does not lead to a palace of wisdom
but a pandemonium of singing, dancing, arguing and fucking,
the LPs jacketless, scattered and stained, the bottles empty,
ashtrays full, as the king bestows upon his queen not royal love
but vicious blows, and in the night the free spirits seem more
like lost souls. Nor is illumination vouchsafed in the rainy grey dawn.
The Sun King, it turns out, is not all that bright, the Master absorbed
in his mistresses, the truth seeker craving the lie of approval,
the substitute father more of a child. And as for the wisdom
of the visiting luminaries - how to gain advances, win awards
and bursaries, build up, then auction your literary 'archive'
('Emory in the States will buy *anything* Irish').
So correspond with the illustrious, though not for
words of wisdom but to push up your price.

It's enough to make anyone abandon the desk …
and seek something substantial, authentic, instead,
like this orange with texture, tang and heft.
Nature loves to make spheres, from the cell to the globe
(and between these the bubble of champagne and elephant turd)
and the unconscious hand makes a sphere when it can,
from scraps of paper, elastic or snot, but loves most a sphere
that fits into the palm, like the *boule* that is perfect in size,
shape and weight, but is hard, cold and pewter-dark grey,
while the orange is soft, warm, effulgent and playful.
It begs to be grasped firmly, rubbed, hefted, squeezed,
and let roll down the forearm, bounced strongly and caught
in a daring punch snatch. Mute, yes, but not inert …
bursting with spirit. Pierce it too roughly and it spits in your eye.
It has to be undone with patience and care - and by hand only,
not sliced by blade. So begin a slow peel at one pole
with a cautious incision by thumbnail, then patient detaching
that brings off the skin whole in one lengthy, unbroken
spiral of zest … though the zest is not just in the skin
but in fibrous flesh, astringent juice. Zest is zen energy,
zenergy … tonic demonic … the zing with a sting.
Drink the juice to be blessed once more by zest.

And here is the return of the ratifying sun to celebrate zest
once again, with a spotlight that picks out the dance of the dust,
the gravity-defying dust that dances and laughs, and flows

round the earth in a perpetual river, blithely violating air space
and territorial waters, and not even *noticing* national borders.

Dust, the symbol of drought, but the bearer of rain
(moisture drops coalesce around tiny dust grains),
dust, the symbol of drouth, but the maker of bubbles
in champagne (they form around specks in the cracks of the glass),
dust, the symbol of death, but the bearer of life
(the river of dust ferries insects, bacteria, seeds, fungal spores).

I will show you the world in a grain of dust, which may have
dropped from cosmic space as gold, diamond, ruby or sapphire dust,
or been violently expelled by volcanoes in Italy, raised in
a whirling dust dervish from desert sands, emitted in China
as industrial gas, or from Golders Green Crematorium
as your manager's ash, be spider legs, nematodes,
mould spores or pollen specks … or shed from your own skin
in tiny flakes. I will show you the world in a grain of dust.
Inside a grain predatory dust mites devour other mites and are
devoured by pseudo-scorpions in turn. I will show you the world
in a grain of dust – because the world once *was* a grain of dust.

In the whirling primordial dust from the stars one minuscule
dust grain attracted another … and then another and another,
till the band of brothers reached 100,000 or so and the dust ball
was just about visible, measuring a tenth of the width of a hair.
And after a century of accumulation, that would please
the severest accountant, it grew to a boulder, a yard wide,
and after another aeon acquired a diameter of a mile
and was promoted again to a planetesimal, a promising
earthlet, an infant earth. Where now is that brave primordial grain?
Deep in the earth's core … or deep in my black heart?
Catching a ride on the dust river, taking the sun in Saharan sands,
or snug in a seabed enjoying a nap? Grain, I salute you, my father
and mother – and also my ubiquitous sisters and brothers,
the twenty-five thousand in this glass of water,
the thousands of others I take with each breath,
and the thousands that dance on in air.

Escaping the drudgery of the lab, he puts to work

his human intelligence at developing the artificial kind.
This is the brave new world of AI. Since mathematical
logic drives science, this must be the way the mind reasons.
No! *Wrong!* As if the dense network of body and mind
could think in a logical straight line. Yet this is the only
paradigm. His intuition is that thought must be always
intuition and that what would be logical is abandoning logic.
But how to express intuition mathematically? Lost,
he abandons his thesis for the Baudelaire solution:
Always be drunk. That's what matters. Get drunk all the time.
And if, on the steps of a palace, in the grass of a ditch, or in
the solitude of a room, you awake to find drunkenness abated,
ask the wind, the wave, a star, a clock, all that sighs, sings
and speaks, flows and flees, ask of these what time it is,
and wind, wave, bird and clock will cry: time to get wasted again.

Then, in the dim upper floor of the bookshop, the slim
Penguin Classics of Chinese poets, wonderfully light in every sense,
as easy to steal as to carry and read. And back at his desk,
now supporting his feet, he embarks on intensive research,
though not into AI but Chinese verse, journeying not into
the automated future but back to twelve centuries earlier
and poets, so intimate and full of zest, they have more
to say than the ponderous solemnities of the Northern
Ireland Renaissance outside the door. Better Po Chü-I
than po-faced locals – Po who goes off madly singing
in the mountains: 'And often, when I've finished a new poem,
alone I climb the road to the Eastern Rock. I lean my body
on the banks of white stone; I pull down with my hands a green
cassia branch. My mad singing startles the valleys and hills.'
Po who sits, dreaming, in idleness: 'Lined coat, warm cap
and easy felt slippers, at the window in the little tower,
sitting by the brazier. Body at rest, heart at peace;
no need to rise early. I wonder if the courtiers
in the Western capital know of these things or not?'
Po who also enjoys wine and does not despise or reject the world,
earning a living as a civil servant: 'In the morning I work
at a Government desk; in the evening I dwell in the Sacred Hills.'
Po who works out a compromise, the life of the half-recluse:
'Mountains are too isolated and bleak; market and court too
deceitful and mean.' But the 'half-recluse' can 'hermitize',
dream in a burrow niche in some undemanding job.

Enter a quest hero home from the quest to enlighten his people.

Stewart, back from American summers of love, in a polka-dot shirt, blue and white striped pants and a big floppy hat barely holding down mad, frizzy hair, that appears to have been electrified by his exuberance and energy, has no illusions as to the difficulty of his task:

'Coming here is like travelling back to the eighteenth century. Was ever a province more provincial?

They hate everything foreign but especially ideas. No one hates ideas more than ideologues.'

And with no illusions on his own status. 'No one here even mentions my writing, much less offers praise.

The one way I could get a swelled head is if someone decided to kick it in. Which of course is highly likely.'

He pauses for a comforting draught of beer (this Master teaches his only student, the trainee quest hero, in the Club Bar).

'Play is the answer,' Stewart announces and playfully pauses to sip from his Smithwick's. 'We learn only through play, the primal impulse of the exuberant cosmos, the animal kingdom, and, even though hidden, of civilisation.

Homo Ludens, Man the Player, has been just as important as Homo Faber, Man the Maker, and Homo Sapiens, Man the Thinker.

Play is how we experiment, discover and change. And play is supralogical, beyond rationality. Homo Ludens includes, but supersedes, Homo Faber and Homo Sapiens.

Once we may have needed philosopher kings - but what we need now are philosopher clowns.'

Pause for another long, bracing draught. 'And no accident that this crucial force shares its name with the fictions presented by actors, the stage play, the screenplay and the television play. These are games with rules that have scarcely changed for two thousand years, works produced by a community of collaborators for a community of spectators … models of wholeness.'

'Poetry was there first.'

'Drama can easily incorporate poetry. The greatest poet ever was a professional dramatist.

In fact I *want* a drama that can accommodate *everything* - poetry and burlesque, the spiritual journey and the glitterball dance, the radical insight and farcical sight gag. Listen, you're a good mimic, with a coarse sense of humour - write a play.'

Therefore the trainee writes a play.

'It's crap,' Stewart sighs.

'Good. I hardly know which side of theatre I despise most - the community of pretentious phoneys who make it, or the community of bourgeois snobs who watch it.'

'You want to be Rimbaud.'

'Po Chü-I.'

'I do know what you mean. When theatre's bad there's nothing worse – and it's nearly all bad. But when it's good there's nothing better.'

'I'd much rather go to the movies.'

'Ah yes ... the musicals. I've just bought the album of Sinatra and Hayworth in *Pal Joey*.'

'*Musicals?*' the trainee shouts in horrified disgust. 'I was thinking of Westerns.'

'Steve McQueen ... a greatly underrated actor ... in *Tom Horn*. At the end, when they're about to hang him, and he looks down from the gallows with calm, magnificent disdain ... *sublime!*'

'Jack Palance as Jesus Raza in *The Professionals* – the revolutionary turned bandit. *The revolu-shay-on, she is like ay woeman. First you love herr because she is beautiful, then you hate herr because she is a horrr.*'

'The revolu-shay-on, indeed,' Stewart sighs. 'It's over, the dream of the sixties. A fatuous decade in many ways.

But for a moment there the youth of the world was one, loving the same music, sharing the same hopes.'

He finishes his pint, sighs, stares down into the empty glass – then rallies, the irrepressible ebullience and fervour returning, crying out with an extravagant gesture as he hands up the glass for a refill:

'GET ME THE GUNS AND I WILL FREE MEHICO!'

But Lao Tzu advises, 'Do that which consists in no
action and order will always prevail.' A wisdom congenial
to those lolling back with their feet on a desk while
neglecting research, and more encouraging still this
explicit rejection of the very idea of research and development:
'Woe to those who wilfully innovate'. Most congenial
of all to one no longer logical is this glad acceptance
of contradiction. 'The Way never acts yet leaves nothing undone.'
This Way is cunningly indirect, moving by parable, paradox,
fable. 'To seek Way is riding an ox to go in search of the ox.'

Learn from water, advises Lao Tzu: 'Nothing in
the world is as soft and yielding as water. Yet for
dissolving the hard and inflexible, nothing surpasses it.
The soft overcomes the hard and the fluid the rigid.'
Water's a teacher, even a Master. 'The highest good is
like water that, without undue striving, brings life to
the ten thousand things. Water flows in places men reject

and so resembles the Way.' Water was dust's unlikely partner.
Dust made the planet but water created the life upon it,
hitching a ride on the dust as ice and biding its time in
the atmosphere, then condensing and falling as rain to
flow in the rivers of Heraclitus down to the oceans of Poseidon.
Water's on the move everywhere, gathering invisibly above
and running secretly below, ubiquitous outside and inside,
two thirds of the surface of earth and much more than two
thirds of ourselves. But what is ubiquitous is soon the familiar
and what is familiar soon taken for granted, making invisible
the mysteries of water, few molecules simpler, yet few
with more complex behaviour. Like dust, it's a shapeshifter
(no other liquid so often and readily cycles from solid to liquid
to vapour), but also a fertiliser, miracle worker (as Holy Water)
… restorer, corroder … renewer, destroyer (when its flow
is curbed or its depths disturbed), accepter, transformer
(nearly universal solvent and catalyst), and a monumental
sculptor (of coastlines and canyons), a child bubble blower
(on rivers and oceans), a filigree maker (of infinitely various
hexagonal snowflakes), an accurate timekeeper (the Chinese
and Greek water clocks), a healer and torturer (for the early
Chinese and the present-day Americans), an uncontainable
escaper and irresistible infiltrator (no roof I have sheltered
beneath has remained waterproof). Water's invasive,
evasive, deceptive, ingenious … and often rebellious,
rejecting its own limitations and rules by refusing to freeze
at zero or to boil at a hundred degrees, becoming instead,
like Sophia Loren, superhot, or, like Cary Grant, supercool.
Intensively studied but not understood. Its fluid dynamics
bamboozled mathematics, and no biologists agree about
what it gets up to inside cells. No passive medium, water's
a key player, part of the action, transforming itself as well
as everything else. And, refusing to behave like other liquids,
when turning solid, freezing, it *expands* (which explains why
my pipes burst last winter) but also gets *less dense* (why ice
does not sink but will float and Titanic did not float but sank).
And the molecule is a volatile, irregular threesome with the Hs
at an angle to the central O, which compensates for being
outnumbered by hogging the bonding electrons, thus making
it negative and the Hs positive, so that all threesome parties
are charged and attract and react with almost everything else.
The molecules even interact constantly with each other in a hectic
3D hokey cokey, except with incessant jostling and jolting,

its perpetually restless partners cutting in and dropping out.
So, at every level, macro to micro, H_2O is all go.

And this dancer is also a teacher, many lessons in its play
between order and chaos and its states of solid, liquid and gas.
Too constrained and we petrify (solid state). Too free
and we vaporise (gaseous state). In between, freedom to flow in
a channel (liquid state). And only the fluid makes beautiful music.
Neither freeze nor vaporise, but cut a channel, flow and sing.

Where is home? A raft on the Heraclitus River – but song
drowns the triumphalist roar of the water. Sing yet more strongly
as the rapids get nearer and the ramshackle raft ever shakier, leakier.
Sing more exquisitely, forcefully, urgently, letting the notes
that have never known gravity soar up from foundering flesh.

What is existence but water in water, the song and dance of vortex
in the song and dance of river? No one knows how, where,
or when life began – but all are agreed that it happened in water.
And God's spirit moved on the face of the waters … and God said
let waters bring forth in abundance the moving creature that hath life.

Attend equally to the taking and giving, the coming and going.
After the mindful eating, mindful excreting, transcendental
defecation, attaining higher emptiness by means of the lower.
Empty bowels, empty mind. Just abide. Take the time.
Feel the space. Time will slow and space increase. Make
a personal spacetime – a portable monk's cell. The life lesson:
be like the cell of an organism, the unit of life, which, instead
of a wall, has a system of membranes, collectively flexible,
finely adaptable and selectively permeable. So it shrewdly assesses
whatever's around it, enriches connexity, develops complexity,
takes what it needs to make energy and blows out the shit.
'Separate and integrate,' counsels the cell, bringing
tension, ambivalence, paradox, 'Protect and connect.'
Remember that street tough who shat himself – dark, semi-liquid
shit running down out of his short trouser leg and clingingly
down his bare thigh, as tears and mucous streaked his face
and he howled in humiliation and rage, running madly past

in the dusk where I stood back discreetly to take it all in,
exulting secretly in his shame. I can still see his brutal face ...
but what was his name? *What was that incontinent bully's name?*

For nearly four billion years organisms happily stayed in the sea.
All in good time, the micromasters advise. Awaiting the gift
of free flow, I recite the Sutra of the Inviolable Moment
and the Sutra of the Immovable Seat. These things, said
Chuang Tzu, are not sure and never swift. Of the ten bald men
nine turned out to be liars, while the tenth remained mute.
Clear-headed amid the five clouds of entanglement,
I play a sweet tune on the noteless flute. All comes
to those who wait – and all goes from those who wait.

In these white shining tiles of our temples of cleanliness,
reflective depths abhorred so reflective surfaces adored,
we see only pure, incorruptible selves. We will cleanse and purge
and live for ever in our decontaminated, gleaming world.
But every breath we take is packed with dust and spores of mould.

After the violent explosions and fireball macrodrama of the stars,
and the astounding creation of life in the seas, there comes
the heroism of the microorganisms who emerged from
the lifegiving waters to make a go of life on rock. The valiant
lichens, hardier even than the Puritan colonists and humbler even
than Catholic saints, symbiotic coalitions of fungi and bacteria,
that learned to survive for long periods with practically no water,
and over aeons colonised and broke down the bleak rock,
crumbling it to make the soil that nurtured plants and then trees.
And the fungi symbiotically joined with the trees to provide them
with roots, strong, dense and deep, interconnected through a vast
fungal network, and then had to learn how to break down
the hard wood they helped to produce ... yet more intensive
research-and-development. More silent teamwork for billions
of years, solving the problem of the oxygen that was toxic by
learning how to breathe the stuff. And then there's all this toxic
calcium living things produce, so hard and therefore so hard
to reduce. Use it for strength. Make a backbone and hard-wearing
brain case – the brain needs protection. Make use of the shit.
Or someone else surely will. There will always be creatures

to eat your shit, as all senior managers know.

Life is a union of symbiotic unions, of shrewd and agile coalitions, a network of networks, a system of systems.

Life is unavoidable motion and change (for resistance to change is itself change - a hardening).

Life is a plenum and also a continuum, and restlessly careers on beyond equilibrium.

Life achieves no stable states but is always like a demented waiter running with a pile of falling plates.

Life is an expert surfer and has learned to ride the flows of energy through the cycles of chemical reactions.

Life needs no designer God but is self-catalytic, autopoietic, a results-oriented self-starter determined to strive and thrive.

Life defies the Second Law of Thermodynamics, creating order out of chaos, the animate out of the inanimate, producing a rabbit from an empty hat.

Life dodges the Law (for a time at least) by making itself an open system that takes in energy (and spews out waste) to maintain a dynamic disequilibrium.

Life is ingenious, resourceful and cunning, an alert and tireless opportunist, never content to *be*, always *becoming*.

Life is always changing shape, direction and tactics (the first grain said, let's get together, the first cell said, let's draw apart).

Life does not believe in mission statement or plan, but will go anywhere that's propitious to do what is necessary with what is at hand.

Life learns to colonise, catalyse, synthesise, in a variety of clever ways self-organise, and make new complex glory emerge.

Life always finds a way. Hey, what's this white stuff? New ice age? I'll just dye the fur, be a polar bear. White is the new brown ... OK?

Life will adopt disguise, improvise, compromise. Can't beat the thing? Be its parasite. Can't eat the thing? Eat its shite.

This is sea? Learn to swim. This is land? Learn to walk. This is air?
Learn to breathe it, get high on it, fly in it. What daring creature
first took to the air, defying gravity, to fly? Was the first attempt
ground up or tree down - leap or glide? Are wings webbed skin
or feathers adapted for flight, in either case a feat of aerodynamic design?
So now a Dreamliner 787 flies 800 overweight creatures at a height
of more than ten thousand kilometres over Dnepropetrovsk, all safe
in a pressurised cabin and compression flight socks and with in-flight
shopping for 'an eye-opening cornucopia of luxury products
and international brands', and a choice of in-flight entertainment:

'Arab sex slaves have seized your young daughter – time for your
secret agent kickboxing skills'. Or: 'When budget cuts threaten activities,
a teacher decides to raise money by learning to be a cage fighter'.
Plied with meals, drinks and snacks (Organic Luxury Multigrain
Crackers with Bega Strong and Bitey Vintage Cheddar, Loacker
Chocolate Sandwich) and each with a screen. 'Secret husband
and wife contract killers are hired to assassinate *each other*. Amazing!'

So, you there, complaining of sameness and staleness, slumped on
the sofa, succumbing to gravity, forfeiting energy, understand that
gravity is always a downer (it just wants *everything* to go downhill)
and that refusing to become is just *so* unbecoming
(what the petrified *do* become are figures of fun). Awake from your
slumber to this stirring truth, that the sameness is not in the world
but in you, that life is not monotony but always neoteny –
a continuous, wild elaboration of the opulent, intricate, complex new.

The Nietzschean nihilists, black hometown cynics who drink
only Guinness, dispute with the socialists drinking blond beer.
As if history has a purpose, a goal! Process is not progress.
The whole thing careers on, with no plan or guiding hand.
The socialists, shouted down, challenge the nihilists –
meet us tomorrow on the field of battle … for a soccer match.
The socialists play soccer every week, follow and analyse the game,
discuss teams and player positions, strategy, tactics and technique.
The nihilists know nothing, never play games, despise sport,
and reject the very concept of team. But refusing a challenge
would make them look weak. Nihilism, strength unassailable,
rejects everything but a challenge. The nihilists, with nothing to lose,
could lose everything. So this is a rabble of individuals versus a team
with a plan, disorderly bottom up versus structured top down.
And after fifteen minutes bottom up are four nil down.
But no belief stronger than believing in nothing. No pride more
fierce than the pride that rejects … and rejects too the ignominy
and shame of defeat. Without knowing the terms, or becoming aware,
the nihilists discover roles, tactics, technique. Stalwart pit pony Bray
is the hero of the day, and becomes, unawares, a defensive midfielder,
who reads play and cuts off advances – none shall pass
or pass the ball – tackling attackers fiercely but cleanly
(the socialists hate to be tackled) and immediately initiating
counter attacks with long, weighted, diagonal passes right

to the toes of running feet. The quest hero finds he can't dribble
or shoot but can run fast and cross the ball. Is also left-footed.
So scoots up and down the left flank … a wingback.
The lumbering socialists can't cope with speed. Wiry, nippy
O'Kane does the same on the right. And Boyle in the centre,
a striker, can score. So out of the nothing comes something, out of
the chaos spontaneous order, out of the shambles self-organisation,
Out of the swarm of individuals a team. Bray the fierce stopper,
unstoppable now, surges forward himself, brushes tackles aside
and thunders a shot that flies over the line before the socialist keeper
even thinks of a dive. The name of the thing is no match
for the thing. Strange complex order emerges from nothing.
The Nietzschean nihilists win seven five.

But remember too the cautionary tale of two cells. Both young,
multi-talented, eager, these equal companions awaited the call.
Then one was sent up to the brain to discover the meaning of life
and the other sent down to the drain to be buried in shite.
One cell was a seer and the other a sewer. This is luck.
This is life. No one said it was fair. (I understood early
that life is unfair - when *The Zombies* only got to ten
with their classic single, *She's Not There*).

Lucky the cells with fulfilling work - neuron and sperm,
so distinct in appearance and skill set but equally keen to connect
and perform. On their joyful journey to the egg a hundred
million hopeful sperm beat their tails in perfect time -
synchronised swimming - and to ponder this wonder
a hundred billion neurons simultaneously link up in
synchronised humming. At the thought of the beloved
and her imminent return, the eager sperm, all hundred million,
wiggle their lithe tails in anticipatory unison, and the neurons
fire together in a hundred-billion-gun salute.

      Praise to the game, elementary particles
      That cooperate in making the chemicals

      That make the cells that make the organs,
      Or instead perform individual functions,

One group permitting you to shoot your load,
Another to think, *Jesus Christ was that good*.

Organismic imperatives – learn, eat, excrete … procreate.
Newton died a virgin, not a feat to emulate. So the hero's
next test in the quest is the sternest – the goddess herself.
Though only a novice goddess, insecure and afraid, ashamed
even of beauty, making a hunch of her exquisite form,
concealing her plenitude in folded arms and letting long hair
fall in front of her face, unsure of allure, but an inferno of need,
and desiring not quest but a nest, not a vain Alan Ladd
but Van Heflin, the dad. Desperate and helpless as Ishtar,
her heart is possessed and her loins are on fire. She must have
the quest hero. Nipples stand forth and a river of lubricant
pours down her thighs, while his cock salmon-leaps in
willingness to oblige, but his head knows all too well
the gravity of this. The quest may be over before it's begun.

Just when he's finally offered a destiny – to collaborate with Jimmy on his
new magazine, to ride forth and vanquish the pharisees and charlatans and Irish
cultural nationalism's many fire-breathing dragons. Scorn will be his bright sword
and insouciance his shield.

Like Stewart, Jimmy wishes to save the province – but Jimmy and Stewart
could never collaborate.

Masters detest each other. '*Him*?' Jimmy says with contempt of his rival
evangelist, 'Is *he* back?'

While Stewart dismisses Jimmy ('a narcissist') along with the other provincial
writers, and needs a break from this province trapped in its past.

'Come with me to the States,' he says to the trainee quest hero. 'I'll get you
a job teaching writing.'

'But I'm a *science* graduate.'

'Don't you love Chinese poetry?'

'And I don't believe writing can ever be taught.'

'But you don't believe in artificial intelligence either.'

'Actually, I do now. Artificial intelligence may be easy enough. It's artificial
common sense that's the difficult part.'

'Think it over anyway. I'm going back in June.'

What does a goddess care for such offers? Her lighthouse nipples
lead him on to his fate and tsunamis of lubricant sweep him away.

But love, for him, is aporetic not operatic – a thing not of passion
but doubt. He puts his whole heart in, he takes his whole heart out,
in, out, in, out. Is love what it's all about? Is Jimmy the Master?
Or Stewart? Is the US the Way? Where shall wisdom be found?

So Li Po comes to the mountain in search of the Master.
Here is the humble hut – but where is the man? He must
have gone higher? But are peaks any closer to heaven?
Does just being cold make a sage? The quest hero
must be alone – but is solitude enough? Anyone can
withdraw in contempt and disgust. 'How must we live?'
cries Li Po once again. 'When we need him the sage
always seems to slip off. The real thing? Or a charlatan?
Both at once – pure peak and dirty pool?' At least this
is a good spot for thinking through to the inevitable nature
of things – light that clarifies, winds that scour, waters that rinse.
A mist hangs on Han river. But clear farther, Hsiang-yang,
Yü-chou and Chung-ling. Journey on. In which sleep tonight?
And remain for how long? A day? Seven weeks? Fourteen
months? Twenty years? Pilgrim with no faith and no
destination, novice with no master, seeker without a Way,
he grips his warped old staff more firmly and walks on.

What if the trainee quest hero had walked on alone
with his staff and his bowl? What enlightenment would he
have known? What sacred Way? What golden fleece?
What holy grail? *What if*? – the cry we must never make
and so always make. What if the matter didn't outweigh
the antimatter? What if the electron was heavier, lighter?
What if the earth didn't tilt on its axis? What if
the sun was hotter, cooler … nearer, farther?
What if he'd gone to the US with Stewart?
Break the art or break the heart? Always the breakages.
Let's break for lunch and break bread, the good solid
sourdough available once again, after the terrible
twentieth century of mass murder, mass entertainment
and the mass-produced, limp, tasteless, textureless,
fragranceless, pallid crap passed off as bread.
Lord, give us each day our daily artisan bread, the crust
hard, almost burnt, rugged and ridged as the primal earth,
but protecting a soft, aromatic pith, an elastic web whose

pockets of gas, the alveoli, hold the rich mixture of scents
released when the bread is ceremonially broken or cut.

    Raising high the breadknife like the sword of Galahad
        I stare fiercely towards the horizon,
           Game as Gilgamesh and Jason.
    Live like a bourgeois and think like a demi-God!

    Why should the settled be sober and torpid?
        Even those who stay at home
           Can make the quantum
    Leap to an excited higher energy orbit.

Energy, that lights the stars, unfurls the flowering, drives
the beasts and makes the heart of matter dance, apply to my mass
the square of c, convert this torpid I to E. For energy is prime mover,
principal shaker, the power that makes the glory, and energy flow
is the river of life. Energy, said Blake, is eternal delight.

For dessert, fruit of legendary heroes, a fig, the most ancient
of all fruits, whose leaf covered Adam's shame (he must
have been well hung), whose tree gave Gautama shade
to come to enlightenment, whose exquisite manner of splitting
moved Marcus Aurelius, and whose syrup moved mother's
recalcitrant bowels. The fruit of paradise, Mohammed sighed,
and a great prophylactic for piles. This one has the weathered
dusty purple-grey of early-church stone and the opulent composure
of an oriental dome, though when squeezed it splits open
to show a dark jam with pale tendrils and hard golden grains,
surprising with contrasts, the sumptuous young woman flesh
and the old-boozer skin, ancient scrotum without and lush vulva within,
yet surprising in unity, an exemplary wholeness permitting consumption
of all of it, flesh, seeds, stalk, skin. Surprising too its birth and growth.
Was ever a flowering concealed … *never seen*, an enclosed *inflorescence*,
the flowers growing *inwards* on the *inner wall* of its syconium …
that a female fig wasp penetrates to pollinate and lay her eggs, which hatch
males and females who immediately mate - whereupon the male,
wingless, blind, small, eats a hole in the wall for the female to fly through
(a rare case of male selflessness) and begin the whole cycle again.
And a tree that can grow anywhere - in a narrow wall crevice or

a rival tree's fork, extending down in search of water adventitious roots.
And every fig tree with its own unique species of fig wasp, one each
for the more than seven hundred varieties – Lemon, Trailing, Creeping,
Weeping … not even psychopathic Strangler fig denied its own wasp.
Learn from the fig to put down roots wherever you find yourself
and flower on the inside, *infloresce* (beautiful concept and beautiful word),
let your female fly free, develop a rich, complex interdependence
like that of the fig wasp and fig tree, and learn from the example of Christ
in the wilderness – bad for once. Hungry and counting on ripe fruit,
he blasted a barren fig tree with a curse: you shall never bring forth
fruit again. This was when Christ became truly a man
and in his hunger and disappointment yielded to spite.
Few remain sweet when the tree bears no fruit.

Now comes the hero's most difficult test. Was there ever a pair
of opposites more completely opposed? No entanglement more
bewildering, no symbiosis more dangerous, no fusion closer to fission,
no unity harder to forge and no process more work to sustain,
than the living together of woman and man. 'Compared to this,'
cries the quest hero in bafflement, 'slaying a dragon's a piece of piss.'
Both terrible and benign is she, like the many-armed Kali
who with one hand gestures gently, 'fear not', and in another hand
brandishes a blade dripping blood, with one hand bestows unique gifts
and in another swings a severed head. Now her beauty, no more
concealed, blooms in the sun, becomes hard to look on like the sun,
striking terror in the hearts of men. If I could see her now as she was
then, emergent in splendour, my old heart would surely stop dead.
Contrarily human, she insists on security but then longs for danger,
looks with disdain upon toiling Van Heflin and then looks around
for a Shane. If you wish to devalue the thing you have, use it,
and if you wish to revalue it, lose it. So *she* falls out of love
with him by winning him and *he* falls into desperate love with her
by losing her. It all changes, even the changeless art. *Shane*,
watched alone, with a bottle of gin, is a tale not of quest hero valour
but middle-aged love. Jean Arthur's loins are on fire for Shane.
Her dull Van is certainly not the man – but she stays with him.
Shane, wounded, rides away.

Now no young Brandon de Wilde, but, ageing, weary, compromised,
waving another gin, 'Fuck off and die, Shane,' he shouts at the screen.
Craven pleading, drunken raging, shameful tears, demeaning lies.
Emotion as futile as rational argument. Each vain attempt only

heightens contempt – with each importuning the Goddess more angry
and loath to oblige. Not the spoils but the toils. Not the gifts but the shifts.
Not the light of the mind but the sweat of the brow. Forget poetry
and think not to lie with the golden queen but mend the fence posts,
feed the chickens, love the bright child, work and sleep.

While off goes Xuanzang on his quest for the scrolls of the Sutras
of Enlightenment, a journey of a hundred thousand leagues
to the west, taking fourteen years, traversing deserts,
scaling mountains, fording rivers, fighting monsters,
braving a multitude of dangers to come at last to the Hill of Life
and receive the scrolls from a Bodhisattva: 'Here is all you need
to know'. Xuanzang opens the scrolls – to find every scroll blank.
The Bodhisattva gaily laughs: 'The seeker learns that everything
is nothing and concludes then that nothing is everything.
Therefore true scriptures are blank.' 'But,' he concedes at once,
'the Middle Kingdom people are foolish and need
an array of imposing books. So take *these* five thousand
and forty eight scrolls, inscribed,' and here he actually guffaws,
'with all the most *beautiful*, most *sacred* words'.

Now the hero departs for the anonymous city, where the shame
is cast off with the name and it is fine to be no one because
no one knows. And in autumn he walks on a grand avenue
where tall, austere apartment blocks face across, sightlessly,
employing that skill of the grand to look upon but never see,
demanding always to be seen, the wrought-iron balconies
for show not use, saying look how we blend strength and filigree
in forms that endure, and imagine the majesty of our dark interiors,
the deep silent stairwells and gleaming curved balustrades.
On this grey day light fades in the late afternoon, the street lamps
slowly lighting up and the chill of the winter to come in the air,
a great many leaves already down but on the august, established
trees many more leaves still disturbingly astir, at once
intimidating and beckoning: *Here you will never be anyone
or anything, never feel at ease or belong, welcome home.*

But what will he do here? What does it matter? Teach,
like the timorous mother and father. The arrogant son
is no braver or better. Besides, doesn't every truth seeker
end up as a teacher? Some people are born to rule, some to

explain the rules. Where will the projectile hit the ground?
What the trajectories of the spheres that collided?
When will the overstretched string at last break?
And what is a true teacher? Someone who knows nothing
… someone with questions not answers … a seeker.

But these teachers are settled and certain, bad tempered, censorious.
These are the Pharisees not the redeemers. Who will teach him
to suffer the teachers? Neither Buddha nor Jesus had colleagues
(disciples are easy). And what are the lessons of this school?
That no one knows less than those sure they know everything,
that none are as inferior as those who think themselves superior,
that no one is weaker than those who crave power, and no one
more dangerous than those who learn righteousness, no one less safe
than the saved, those convinced they know what you should do,
who if able would force you to do it and gladly destroy you
should you refuse, those so swift to criticise, and swifter still
to take offence if criticised themselves, who think anger is noble,
a sign of integrity, the justified wrath of the elect of God.
Was there ever an angry Awakened One?

I inform you conclusively that there are no conclusions.
I tell you with certainty there can never be certainty.
'What is more necessary than seeking truth?' the Philosopher
King enquired. 'Never to find it,' answered his Fool.

At a table by the window in the staffroom sits the quest hero,
trapped behind a leaning tower of exercise books, and assailed
by the babble of Babylon, believing that he and not one among these
is the anointed of God. 'Lord, innumerable evils have compassed
me about. Oppressors seek after my soul and whisper together
against me in hate. Let their way be slippery and dark,
that they see not, and make their loins continually to shake.
Lord, my heart is sore pained within me. For I sink in deep mire.
I sink, lost and forgotten as the dead out of mind. Attend now to my cry.
Bring me up unto thy holy hill. Compass me about now with songs
of deliverance.' Thus he prays by the window in his only free hour,
till the deputy head interrupts his psalm: 'Mrs Wagstaff has
a terrible migraine. Would you mind taking Home Economics with 4a?'

Dusty, exhausted, the quest hero reaches the river and cries out,
'Ferryman, take me to the other side'. The sun-weathered ferryman,
shading his eyes: 'For me you are already on the other side.'
'My journey has been arduous and perilous and has no end in sight.
Do not further weary me. Ferry me.' 'But where will the end be?
The cheating horizon is always retreating, at the turn of the bend
is another bend.' Nevertheless, the ferryman rows his boat over
and carefully studies the dust-covered wayfarer. 'Not many quest
heroes make it this far.' 'Devoured by the fire-breathing dragons?'
The ferryman solemnly shakes his head: 'Lured by the Goddess
with loins on fire.' 'Hard indeed is the way, with many dangers
and snares. But how can you endure to go back and forth, back
and forth, over the same stretch of river?' 'No one ever crosses
the same river twice. The dancing current never takes the same
path twice. Besides, at no time may we escape from ourselves –
a constraint tested constantly and needlessly by hauling the cage
from place to place. It is only within ourselves that we move,
invisible and mercurial, like the laughter of the current
in the torrent of the river.' 'I perceive indeed, ferryman, that you
have become wise. But what lies across on the far side?
More rivers? More dragons? What shall I find?' 'There lies
the limitless desert, the kingdom of dust, where, over the bones
of lost seekers, the faceted eyes of dark insects keep watch.'

In the desert of the middle years wanders the quest hero,
hungry and thirsty, denied recognition and love,
Every manuscript returned with a tiny rejection slip
and the Goddess wrapped in cerements entombed beneath
the sand. Failed as a scientist. Failed as a mathematician.
Failed as a nihilist. Failed as a quest hero. Failed as a writer.
Failed as a lover. Failed as a failure. No heresiarch burning,
no Icarus drowning, no garret seer starving, just a schoolteacher
climbing the scales. *Mediocre*. Not the grandeur of despair,
the blasted heath and howling gale, but the workaday nausea
of disappointment, as banal as going bald. Slowly the hero
loses faith, and with it direction, identity, substance
… a blown husk increasingly one with the dust,
as the apparently identical days and years dimly drift past,
with energy waning and gravity winning, the dragons not slain
but updated, with refitted claws and enhanced breath of fire.

The dragon of blame that seeks scapegoats to hate – the fearful parents, gruelling work, demanding queen.

The dragon of resentment that poisons the brain, the dragon of stinginess that hardens the heart.

The twin dragons, disgust and self-pity – disgust for the venal age and pity for the sensitive soul forced to suffer it.

The dragon of lust, long repressed, turning sour, the dragon of wrath that would smite the vain, and worse even than rage,

The dragon of envy that in secret shame covets the fame of the prospering charlatans he claims to despise.

Did you believe that grains of sand are self-contained,
serene worlds? These are the lost souls, buried in hell,
deprived forever of the attention of God. In the desert
every grain of sand howls for a Blake.

Failure can never go home – that would worsen the shame –
but must journey on over the desert, though aware that
the desert has no end, no gifts to bestow and no truths to impart.
Failure is the acid of embitterment that eats out the heart,
and the miasma of rancour that envelops the mind.
No, failure is not envy, rage or despair. Failure is absolute
featurelessness – the certainty that nothing is happening
or can happen. Failure is a February four o'clock pewter,
a deadly pall over all heaven and a dearth over all the rich land
where the trees have been stripped bare and, hunched dead
and black like burnt matches, no more flare and billow,
where the sky is a curdled grey, ground hard as iron ore,
and the Heraclitus River is entirely frozen over,
where ice grips the waters, the earth … and the heart.
There will come no redeemer. Nor any deliverance.
In the night runs the sore and ceases not.

Instead of the process, petrifaction.
Instead of the unity, fragmentation.
Instead of belonging, alienation.
Instead of eternity, acid time.

Time – the thing we invoke most but understand least,
The inscrutable unmoved mover, demiurge of the dust.

Time is no inert background, no docile dimension.
Time is the thing itself, process and action,

A demonic illusionist who contracts and expands,
Flies … or hangs on your hands,

Makes your yesterday dim to a distant grey blur
But brings childhood increasingly close and clear,

Speeds up what you love and slows down what you hate,
When you yourself slow down, begins to accelerate,

Lets only those who don't have it know it, relishing the joke
Of teaching time-wealth management to the terminally broke.

Even his pupils are ageing now. In a station he recognises
a girl, once a beauty, voluptuous even at fifteen,
and haughty in the certainty that the world would submit
to her, but now shapeless, overweight, poorly dressed,
blotchy and vexed in the crush of the ordinary.
He begins to move discreetly away - but then sees
that she can see no one. The eyes, once so cool and assured,
are blind with bafflement and fear. It is still new and strange
to her, the shock of the years and the indifferent world,
that not merely no more a princess, she can count for
so little - and ahead just this trudge through a desert,
the mocking, cavorting dust, hunger and thirst.

It is always only a question of time, the mystery
none may ever know, the tyrant none may overthrow.
Time is the maker and time is the breaker. Time is
the life force and time is the death wish. Time is
freedom, time is fate. Time is God and time is Satan.
And as Satan's neatest twist is to make us believe
he does not exist, so time can make time appear to stop,
malevolent, insidious, whispering, 'Develop a personal
indifference to match the indifference of the world.

Since the world takes no interest in you, take no interest
in it, never venture, engage, discuss, bend (in any sense,
literal, figurative). Surrender to gravity. Retreat to
a comfortable orbit, from TV to kitchen and back to TV.'

It was TV that made the tough (what was his name?)
shit himself, too absorbed in the power of the street's first TV
… in worldly, swanky (slightly trashy) McCrossan's,
who were happy to leave their curtains open
and let a multitude, open-mouthed, stand in their garden,
all distinctions – of age, class, gang and gender – now forgotten,
all still and silent, lost in wonder. For they know that a new God
has come among them and that they have gladly become its
creatures and will forever be in thrall, heedless of dark and cold,
bowel and bladder, worshipping the phosphorescent God
of the twilight. As light fades, silently the faithful gather …
and look in rapture on the face of God, the black and white
circles and squares of inscrutable Test Card C.

But time the deceiver promotes the illusion of a permanent self
in a changeless environment where nothing is happening,
so that time can get on with its work in secret, the minuscule
changes, continual but invisible, the mighty time-defying pillars
weakened by every termite nibble – till suddenly, shockingly,
they fall. Bit by bit he tires of complainers and whingers.
What are the Psalms but poetic whingeing? *I'm much too special
to languish in exile. The anointed of God is entitled to better.*
Bit by bit he tires of contempt and disgust (but develops
new contempt and disgust for TV). Contempt and disgust
lead to torpor and tedium, Flaubert's complaint
that he's too bored to summon the strength to stand up.

Salvation is always in walking. And today is a day for
the heavy shoes. Like an old married couple who have walked
the same roads side by side for many decades or waited together,
learning patience, each shoe is bent, wrinkled, discoloured,
and spotted, and gives off the musty smell of geriatric genitals.
But they offer traditional, laced-up commitment rather than
the modern come and go of the slip-on (which ought to be
known as the slip-off). Tightening the laces gives the symbiotic

unity of content and form, like passionate emotion bound up in
a sonnet or the lax warmth of a women's body laced in a corset.
When shoes are laced tight they regain their authority.
Leather soles and heels make a purposeful clack that announces
someone sure of destination and way, and shod strongly
enough to deliver, if blocked by some aggressive brute,
an accurate and salutary kick in the balls.

Ah but the rain is like Irish rain – iron rods of God wrath
to punish the weak earth, the wayward, indulgent, sinful earth.
Already the puddles are many and large and the drops that fall
from gutters make concentric spreading rings, and here
a bubble forms and darts adroitly round a puddle … insouciant
gaiety getting away with it. Ah no, it takes a direct hit. *Ouf!*
Always a bubble willing to risk it – to grow and float, glitter
and dance, defy, albeit briefly, and die. And earth too responds with
the running water music, the bewildering antics of fluid dynamics
that for centuries mystified physics. So science learned never
to step in the Heraclitus River and risk being drowned in
the craziness of flow. As the great Werner Heisenberg said on
his deathbed, 'I have only one question for God: *Why turbulence?*'

Heavy shoes, coat, and the staff of this seeker – a telescopic
button-operated umbrella. I peel off the cover that's tight as
a condom, press for the always surprisingly fast whoosh and thump
as the spokes rise and spread to the full, and I brace for the recoil
kick of a gun and the exhilarating snap and tug of sail in the wind.

Forth once again with their staffs they go, pondering, sounding the good
earth for grounding and counsel.

'If I describe my staff as a short staff,' notes Tokusan, 'I deny it reality. 'But in
refusing it description I deny it recognition.'

Strolling together by the river, thoughtfully weighing staffs as they pace, the
Masters consider this conundrum in silence.

At last Funyo sighs: 'If a man could truly know what the staff is, his study of
Zen would be complete.'

Cho of Rokutan is deeply shocked by such presumption: 'If a man thinks he
knows what the staff is, he will fly like an arrow straight to hell.'

Nevertheless, Hyakujo speaks with a firm voice: 'My staff supports unstable
heaven and keeps clinging earth in its place.'

But E-myo cries, with a vehemence surprising in one so serene: 'All that the staff keeps in place is the grasping right hand.'

At which Kokushi stops and plants his staff on hard earth. 'If the question is sand in a bowl of boiled rice, the answer is staff on the river path.'

All also stop to observe his staff, drawing their thin robes more closely about them in the cold wind that sweeps down the river.

Ho-an, the ninth patriarch, has thus far been mute, so that all turn at once when he clears his throat.

'If a man truly knows what the staff is, let him take it up and lean it on the tree over there.'

Join me now in the walker's hymn. I will *walk* to find redemption.
I will *walk* to find grace. I will *walk* to be saved. I rejoice
in the Church of the Holy Walker, its sacred texts those of
the walking quest heroes from Li Po to Basho to Thoreau,
and even that lunatic Rimbaud, the cross-country walker
who crossed entire countries on foot, barely pausing to eat,
so incessant the seeking that soon became fleeing:
'I haven't found what I want. I won't stay here long.'
Everywhere indolent, compromised, venal. Across
the disappointing continents he walked, on and on,
never knowing what he was seeking - but driven.
The less clear the grail the more frantic the quest.
I have drawn on his energy, stolen his fire, used his
frog's legs to lengthen and strengthen *my* stride.

Hey, let's have a frog as the Walker Church symbol -
squat, goitrous, with sixty-a-day croak and shopping-bag
eyes, its entire body one fearful thumping heart,
but game enough to go caducibranchiate, shed gills
and breathe air, become our precursor, one of the first
and most valiant quest heroes, using its long, Nijinsky
legs to heave up and out of familiar warm slime
and walk on the cold, strange and perilous earth.

And the John the Baptist of the Walker Church is
Australopithecus afarensis, who decided to rise on
hind legs and become the first creature to walk upright,
the bent back and spine growing straight, the pelvis
that pointed down at the ground turning round to

become a vase, calyx, thrusting up to the light the strong
stem of the torso and neck and the flower of the head,
like the palm tree that won't waste its energy branching
but soars up as far as it can to explode in a firework display
of bright green. So now *Homo erectus*, the uplifted,
blossoming head taking in the whole scene, the thrillingly
panoptical view from on high, learns the joys
of bipedalism, the awareness, the knowledge, the wonder,
the freedom, the lure of the mystic horizon, and the hands
now released for expression, the beginning of language,
the free hand that rises to point out, *Sheez!* Just look
at *that*! – and then turns back to beckon, *Cmon!*

But let us worship no icon, submit to no doctrine,
aspire to no paradise, kneel at no shrine.
Salvation is not an endstate but a process.
Be on your way, pilgrim. Walk on to go back, to restore
the lost unity of the trinity of equals – mind, body and world.
All holy walkers restore the lost unity. Walk to recover
the primal state. Not just to *be* … but belong and behold
and become and beget … to partake and flow.
Walk to be process i.e. without purpose, alone, monad nomad,
the mind and the body unburdened, the mind embodied
and the body embedded, everything densely and finely connected.
Swing limber limbs to link body and mind, to alert all the sensors
and ready the brain, to plug the pleasure dome of your
neural connectome into the great pleasure dome of the world,
and synchronise the dance of your hectic thought
with the hectic dance of the universe, the antic
ontic interdependence of everything.

Sing with me now. I detach to engage. I submerge to emerge.
I'm alone to be one with the many. I walk to become the still centre.
I become insignificant to burn with significance. I reject power
to blaze with the power and the glory. I repudiate divinity
to make life divine, declare meaninglessness the new meaning
in the democratic kingdom of arrogant humility where paradox
abdicates the better to reign, each is never and always the same,
it is always the right time for never the right time, and the knowing
looks of those who know nothing meet the puzzled gaze
of those who know far too much. So I walk in airy earthiness,

knowing naivety, hectic serenity, effortless striving, tragic zest.

Here the shower is brightly over and a cleansed sky reflected
in radiant pools. Relieved clouds and the redolent earth
are renewed, for a moment the possibility space is
illuminated and everything possible is *brilliantly* possible
in the bright hush of imminence after the rain.

Then *Homo erectus* became *Homo sapiens*, walker
and talker, who led a group into the dangerous unknown,
from the bountiful savannahs to the cold, wet north,
repeatedly telling them, we must never be comfortable,
for comfort makes lazy and stupid, but hunger and danger
make leaner and stronger, make us grow smarter, live longer.

But eventually *Homo sapiens* tires and settles down
by the tireless river and learns to till the fertile earth.
Then the city emerges – and self-organises. The little
settlements by the river bit by bit grow together
and at last coalesce to create the Uruk of Gilgamesh,
who surrounds the 80,000 souls with walls, provides
them with water by cutting canals, and so creates
the first cell of civilisation, the city, a populous cell
with these new creatures, citizens, who evolve in
ceaseless interaction and at last become aware of
themselves, and hence of others: If *I* am bewildered
and fearful then *they* must be too. So the citizens
are obliged to conclude, with a sigh, that they do
unto others what they wish others do unto them,
the duty of human maturity that emerges simultaneously,
though separately, in China, Judea, India and Greece.

The urge is to stay clear, above and apart.
But enlightenment for one consigns the others to the dark.
Buddha abandoned wife and child. So did Dessie McBride.
We are one people, tortured and torturing, haunted by questions.
How much to give to the others and how much to keep?
When to be stubborn and when to surrender?
Is *Good question* always the only good answer?

No clear answers here in the tumultuous city
that has never heard of moderation, logic or consistency,
with *The Smoker's Paradise* next to *Cancer Research*,
and in front of the *Everything-For-a-Pound* shop a tub
of brooms at £5.00. Here disorder makes order, the presence
of strangers protects you from strangers, anonymity
lets you be someone and crowds make you fully alone.

Remember that Rome invented concrete and glass
and had high rises (the forty six thousand up to
seven storey *insulae*), immigrants (six to eight of every ten
from outside Italy), fast food stalls (on every corner *popinae*),
crass entertainment, baths, brothels, divorcees and casual sex
in graffitied alleys with cocks and cunts scrawled on the walls.
Then regard not with disgust but with wonder the splendour
that burgeons before you. This is the glory that was Rome.

The city sets you free - but then enslaves you in desire.
The city blesses you with bounty - but makes you cry *More*!
The city gives you home - but also a burning urge to roam.
The city confers anonymity - but only in order to win renown.
The city makes you learn - but learn how little you know.
The city draws you to its lights - but quickly leaves you in the dark.
The city is Prometheus, thief of fire - but is also the eagle.
(The city tears out its own guts - but regrows them at once.)
The city created king and priest - but then rejected king and priest.
The city created the automobile - but is now rejecting the automobile.
The city let its centre die - but now has brought it back to life.
The city spreads, soars high, digs deep - but never knows what it seeks.
The city strives to be complete - but dies the moment it succeeds.

And the hierarchy gets light in its lofty head and begins to
believe it is *all* in the head. Descartes detaches his head
from his body and holds it aloft as the wonder of Europe,
declaring, 'I think, therefore I am'. The body just a device
for supporting this head as it works out the mechanism
of the clockwork universe, and Newton's laws explain
the motion of the toy wound up by God and left to trundle

around predictably in Descartes's grid of space and time.
'Science,' predicted Descartes, will make us 'the Lords
and Masters of Nature', thus detaching not merely the head
from the body but the body and head from the whole thing,
making the relation to it instrumental, the wish
not to belong and serve but rule and enslave.

But then rose up a saviour – the extraordinary figure
of Gottfried Wilhelm Leibniz, who strove harder than anyone
to understand unity: 'The universe – whatever it is –
is a unified whole, like an ocean; even the smallest movement
will extend its influence to any distance, however great.'
But as everyone is immersed in the ocean no one can have
a complete view of this whole; there are only the countless
partial views: 'Just as the same city viewed from different
directions appears entirely different and, as it were, multiplied
perspectively, in the same way, because of the infinite
multitude, there are just as many different universes,
which are, nevertheless, only perspectives on one.'

Newton and Leibniz, the polar opposites, everything
proposed by Newton contradicted by Leibniz.
No things without space. No space without things.
The void must be empty. The void can't be empty.
No events without time. No time without events.
Everything is independent. Everything is connected.
Everything is determined. Everything is contingent.
The whole thing is planned. The whole thing evolves.
Everything is mechanism. Everything is organism.
Nothing is novel. Everything is novel.
Everything has substance. Nothing has substance.
Things make processes. Processes make things.
Causation is linear. Causation is circular.

Did Newton's view prevail because relationism is difficult
– who wants entanglements running in circles?
And because of the yearning for the absolute and permanent,
the immutable backdrop of space and time?

In the Leibniz philosophy of dependent autonomy
the parts remain autonomous while belonging to the whole
and the whole becomes autonomous though made entirely of parts.
So the parts can all party while the whole remains holy.
And there is no superior, no inferior, no foreground, no background,
no inside, no outside, no centre, no edge - there is only the skein,
the web, the mesh. And time is freed from Newton's clock,
space from Newton's empty grid, intelligence from logic's cage,
the laws from timeless truth's deep freeze (yes, even the laws
evolve, even the laws can change) and the universe
from the centralised planning of God. Now all the cells
and the particles may join hands once more. And the galaxies
and stars and all the organisms of the earth may rejoice,
for everything is free to improvise the great dance in time.

Around and around goes the great dance, becoming more
structured and sophisticated, inventing, creating and self-organising
- as atom, molecule, cell, organism, city, society, planet, star,
galaxy, universe - dizzying the rationalist by spinning in circles
and rejecting distinctions of mover and moved, beginning and end,
cause and effect, this changing that which changes this which
changes that in a circular ballet of tit for tat and tat for tit,
as around and around and around it goes, with rings on its fingers
and bells on its toes, and what it all means no one knows,
except that to think straight we must think in circles.
Feedback is what makes the world (and my head) go round
in beginningless riddles of egg and chicken, chicken and egg,
the brain body's servant but also its master, an effect of complexity
but also its cause, and the only solution to the growing complexity
is roasting the chicken and frying the egg for the energy to marvel
again at the whole thing, its purposeless majesty, fecund
contingency, profligate novelty, a wanton child, heedless,
wishing only to play, caring nothing for what it accidentally makes,
throws away and forgets, demanding imperiously *More! More!*

It is never the world but the chroniclers who grow weary, worn out
    By novelty, energy, contrariness - and begging
For mercy ... a slowdown, a break ... as if *anything* could regulate
    The swarming, connecting, reacting, relating,
        Enfolding, unfolding, emerging ... *creating*
            Of the turbulent flux and flow

That left God for dead long ago.
Too much is never enough for the whole thing.

Capacious, capricious, inventive, deceptive, it loves to mutate
    And confound all prediction, insisting
That no same is ever the same because no circumstances repeat,
    And then doubling back in a cunning U-turn
      (Will the post-postmodern be pre-premodern?)
        Or like the psycho in a horror movie
        Seem dead to jump back more cruelly.
Too much is never enough for the whole thing.

Not even the madly expanding immensity of the universe will suffice
    For the ravening, burgeoning and ramifying
That brooks no check or choice. Only a multiverse has enough space
    To reject either/or and not defer or foreswear.
      Everything possible must happen somewhere.
        In parallel worlds on roads not taken,
        All the lost lives shine and beckon.
Too much is never enough for the whole thing.

Do we really need leather-look nail varnish, apophatic theology,
    Eggs-and-bacon ice cream, ambush marketing,
The Book of Russian Criminal Tattoos, microcosmic ontology,
    Welsh peat bog snorkelling, intelligent toilets,
      Coffee beans passed through bowels of civets,
        Mandarin and tonka bean scented candles?
        YES - and self-sterilising door handles.
Too much is never enough for the whole thing.

It is always evolving, Darwin explains, overthrowing the tyranny
of essence and permanence, and acknowledging the power
of the minuscule and gradual. Nothing is absolute, nothing eternal.
Everything living mutates, adapts, dies, and all that is purposeful
and mindful is a consequence of forces that were purposeless
and mindless. But the natural move is to move beyond nature.
So values evolve. Obligation evolves. And finally
freedom evolves, to clash with obligation and live with it
in a far-from-equilibrium, always difficult, tension.

The evolution of Darwin himself should inspire slow developers,

the apparently idle and dim-witted son of a country doctor who
complains to him bitterly, 'You care for nothing but shooting, dogs,
and rat-catching, and you will be a disgrace to yourself and your family.'
A country doctor or a country parson? Neither inviting.
Then contingency offers a chance to evolve, a post on a survey ship,
the HMS Beagle, as 'captain's dining companion' (there is one
falling out, over slavery, which Darwin abhors, and the two agree
not to discuss it). But the youthful diversion, the jolly adventure,
becomes soon a quest for the meaning of life. In the course
of the voyage Darwin sails, walks, observes, marvels, ponders,
takes numerous samples, makes copious notes, And gradually …
gradually … there grows on him his theory of gradual process.

Nature, never replete, seeking always to procreate, restless
and curious, ceaselessly roams in the adjacent possible,
and, never content with the making, is always adjusting,
tinkering, tweaking, using what was intended for one thing
to do something else, so that feathers become wings, and fins
become limbs in novel stranger variations, win a few,
lose a few, dump, recycle, rethink, trial and error the smartest
researcher, in play that has no end but love of the process,
like sunlight that dances on waters that flow.

On the *Beagle* Darwin studies the ship, sea and sky. Is that
mast pennant dirtier now? Down with it for examination.
Covered in dust that includes spores, bacteria, pollen grains,
silica, soil particles. He is first to discover the river of dust
that connects the processes of Africa with the processes of
the Americas - the nurturing dust that is not death but life.
And as though to confirm this hypothesis a living
grasshopper drops out of the sky to the deck at his feet.
Everything is linked and life is always on the move.
Such bounty and beauty! It all connects.

'You cannot imagine how pleased I am,' he writes to a friend,
'that the notion of Natural Selection' is 'a purgative
on your bowels of immutability'. This discovery of transformation
will transform in turn the human world, teaching it humility.
'In the beginning,' spake Darwin the prophet, 'was the parasitic bug.'
It is not that the whole thing is like a machine and we resemble it

but that *we* are living organisms and the whole thing resembles *us*: 'There is a simple grandeur in this view of life … being originally breathed into matter under one or a few forms … that from so simple an origin, through the process of gradual selection of infinitesimal changes, endless forms most beautiful and most wonderful have evolved.' This may well be the most important insight of science – though President Thomas Bell, of the Linnaean Society, which published Darwin's revolutionary paper, complained in the Society's Journal that the year had not been 'marked by any of those striking discoveries which at once revolutionise the department of science on which they bear'.

But in Europe rigid hierarchy has come to prevail and to petrify even the exuberant cities so that the lower levels of the hierarchy migrate to the new world, infusing it with energy and producing the exemplary American affirmers.

Let the world resound again with those mighty names – Emerson, Thoreau, Melville, Whitman and William James, who said, 'The mood of a Schopenhauer or Nietzsche … though often an ennobling sadness, is almost as often only peevishness … The sallies of the two German authors remind one … of the shriekings of two dying rats.'

And James also said, 'To the jaded and unquickened eye it is all dead and common, pure vulgarism, flatness … disgust …

What is life on the largest scale, Schopenhauer asks, but the same recurrent inanities? Yet of the kind of fibre of which such inanities consist is the material woven of all the excitements, joys and meanings that ever were, or ever shall be, in this world.'

'I embrace the common,' Emerson said, 'I explore and sit at the feet of the familiar, the low.'

These Western affirmers, like the old Eastern Masters, rejected logic. 'A foolish consistency is the hobgoblin of little minds,' said Emerson. 'Do I contradict myself?' Whitman asked. 'Very well then, I contradict myself.'

And their most affirmative contradiction – to be at the same time sublimely transcendent and resolutely down to earth, equally in love with the ideal and real, what is over the head and beneath the feet. Emerson's coffee mug maxim: 'Hitch your wagon to a star.'

Do not the canonical sources agree? Of one voice, the old Eastern Masters, new Western affirmers.

Emerson: 'The only prophet of that which must be, is the great nature in which we rest as the earth lies in the soft arms of the atmosphere;

That Unity … within which every man's particular being is contained and made one with all other …

We live in succession, in division, in parts, in particles. Meantime within man is the soul of the whole;

The wise silence; the universal beauty, to which every part and particle is equally related; the eternal ONE.'

And this unity is process: 'There are no fixtures in nature. The universe is fluid and volatile … Everything looks permanent until its secret is known.'

Whitman, the poet of creation and unity: 'Always the procreant urge of the world … Always the knit of identity.'

'We live, as it were, upon the front edge of an advancing wave', explained William James.

'And our sense of a determinate direction in falling forward is all we cover of the future of our path.'

For chance is the only creator … selector, rejecter, combiner, refiner
… most thoughtless and yet most intelligent designer.
'Let us not fear to shout it from the house-tops if need be,'
shouted William James, 'for we now know that the idea of chance
is, at bottom, exactly the same thing as the idea of gift …
its presence is the vital air which lets the world live.'

The despisers despairing, the affirmers aspiring.
The despisers dyspeptic, the affirmers appetitive.
The despisers fastidious, the affirmers omnivorous.
The despisers withdrawing, the affirmers engaging.
The despisers disdaining, the affirmers praising.
The despisers deflating, the affirmers aerating.
The despisers dissecting, the affirmers connecting.
The despisers rigid, the affirmers fluid.
The despisers holding, the affirmers flowing.

These affirmers had the nerve to admire and risk appearing naïve
(it is always sophisticated to sneer and simple-minded to cheer),
to be happy and risk seeming soft in the head, to be passionately
eloquent and risk sounding ridiculous, to fly at the sun
and risk falling like Icarus. And their books developed bottom-up,
evolving as exuberantly and messily as life, and never final,
never finished. 'God keep me from ever completing anything,'
Melville cried in *Moby-Dick*, 'This whole book
is but a draught - nay but a draught of a draught'.

And they read, thought and wrote with such passionate urgency,
as though lives depended on this, which they did. So intense
their bewildering, brief, only lives. 'I love my fate,'
wrote Thoreau, 'to the very core and rind'. The Americano:
equal portions of passion, energy, eloquence, exaltation and zest.
With strong infusions of humour and a crucial dash of craziness.
'I caught a glimpse of a woodchuck,' admitted Thoreau,
'and felt a strange thrill of savage delight, and was
strongly tempted to seize and devour him raw;
not that I was hungry then, except for that wildness ...'

Drink a strong Americano and return to the factory settings.
Reenergise, refesh, review, renew, rebut, reboot.
This Irish quest hero will not be, like others, an embittered
old teacher. He will not petrify like so many old men.
He is petrified of being petrified, scared stiff of becoming
irremediably stiff. He will not harden, rage and rant,
but teach whatever shit they want as though it is news
of the return of the Messiah. He will shine like a quasar.
He will whirl like a dervish. He will burn with a deviant
energy that would inspire even cynical Irish. Any shit is
compelling when it catches fire. And likewise any teacher.
It is not *what* is taught that counts but *how* – the rigour and energy,
the style of delivery. The lesson is the teacher, a way of looking
at the world ... and therefore of grasping and changing the world.
He will be an exemplar of transformation. He will change
both by fire and by air – conflagrate and aerate, going into
each class with a vibrant delight that will make the most flame-proof
material ignite and the flattest of flat bouncy castles inflate.
It is always personal. The writer is the message, the priest
is the religion, the doctor is the medicine, and the teacher
is the lesson. As mother insisted, time and again,
it is never what but who you know that really counts.

And the task is to render experience vivid. Walk, see, feel
and think like the US affirmers. Thoreau: 'I walk every day
about half the daylight.' Emerson: 'Crossing a bare common,
in snow puddles, at twilight, under a clouded sky, without
having in my thoughts any occurrence of special good fortune,
I have enjoyed a perfect exhilaration. I am glad to the brink of fear.'

Whitman, the Yankee quest hero, walked every day in
an open-necked shirt on the open road (in reality the streets
of New York, in a coat). William James walked himself into his grave.
First he climbed Mount Jo and then took the Indian Trail
on an eight-and-a-half-hour walk that made him feel his
'good old solid elastic internal tone'. Next a seven-hour walk
to Lake Golden and back via Avalanche Pass. But on the hike
after that he lost his way and was obliged to make a thirteen-hour
detour that damaged his great heart beyond repair.

I should have gone with Stewart to the promised land, the States.
Drunk the heady Americano and experienced the high of
affirming the low. No, no, no, no. Strike that from the record.
Select and delete. No regrets. For even the promised land
knows no rest. Even those in the promised land are driven
to quest – Ahab's black grail of the white whale.

South east from Nantucket sails the Pequod, down across
the Atlantic, round the perilous Cape, then north east
through the Crozetts towards Java and the Malacca Straits,
turning south east once more, past Sumatra and Timor,
by the Straits of Sunda to the China Seas and into the Pacific
to meet its fate, encountering, along the way, icebergs and ice,
yellow meadows of brit, enchanted becalmments, raging gales,
the mysterious giant squid, teeth-tiered sharks, tormented leviathans,
and the eerie, demonic beckoning of the spirit spout in the night.
The bleakest quest saga, most gorgeously told, the inexorable
rhythm of the sumptuous sentences lifting and carrying,
gently but strongly, as the swell of the lambent southern ocean
lifted and drove the Pequod: 'Forward through the sparkling sea
shoots on the gay, embattled, bantering brow.'

And the first awareness of the madness and futility of the quest:
'But in pursuit of those far mysteries we dream of, or in tormented
chase of that demon phantom that, some time or other, swims
before all human hearts; while chasing such over this round globe,
they either lead us on in barren mazes or midway leave us whelmed.'
The first suspicion that God is a prankster and the cosmos his prank:
'There are certain queer times and occasions when a man takes
this whole universe for a vast practical joke, though the wit

thereof he but dimly discerns, and more than suspects
that the joke is at nobody's expense but his own.'

But here is an island out of time. No dreadful past to haunt
and taunt, no merciless future to age and degrade. No weather,
no disturbance. No corruption, no decay. Not even the temperature
and light will change. Here all is calm, all is cool, all is bright.
The trays of luscious produce gleam, the cabinets serenely hum.
The freezers have frozen time itself. We famished mariners who
never found the blessèd isles may sail these blessèd laden aisles,
and at the helm on the high and wide back end of a mighty
container ship made of wide mesh to make thrillingly visible
to all at sea the riches piling up like nature's bounty in the hold.
Not bounty but booty. Not cargo but spoils. We are plundering
Vikings on a raid and should have a prow with a warrior-maiden
figurehead. Orange juice, multi-grain cereal, artisan bread,
noodles, tiger prawns, carrots and spring onions, mixed leaves
of rocket, pea, spinach and cress (the plant of immortality
that eluded Gilgamesh) ... and of course yet more fruit
(by their five fruits a day ye shall know them, the responsible ones).
But here bloom the flowers of the lotus that sigh, *brother mariners,*
rest ye from toil. Does a Viking cook? Here are feasts fit for royalty
requiring no work. I hear the siren song of the ready meals
but keep my head. Could a process philosopher buy processed food?
I sail past - and pass too the *Eat Natural* bars, whose rich mulch
of berries and hazelnuts rests on dark chocolate. Yield no advantage
to gravity. Hardy quest heroes must keep down their weight.
Resolute at the helm, in spite of a three-for-two offer on bars
(cunningly next to the checkout ... the bastards) and a stubborn
wheel that pulls left, I stand, strong and virile but chaste,
and steer straight, as, like a yearning lover waiting in port,
a woman reaches out and waves, and a voice
from on high cries, *Cashier number eight.*

The mad quest through the jest of the world must itself be the grail.
Melville, a great object-oriented ontologist, loved, and described lovingly,
every thing on that ship - the mat, line, crotch, monkey-rope, try-works,
tub, tun, buoy, dart, waif-pole and warp - and, also a processist, loved
every task - the blacksmithing, carpentry, cooking and sailing,
harpooning and chasing, securing and hoisting, cutting and firing.
The sublime, secret pleasure of squeezing the lumps in the whale sperm

to fluid: 'A sweet and unctuous duty! ... Such a delicious mollifier!
As I bathed my hands among those soft globules ... as they richly broke
to my fingers, and discharged all their opulence, like fully ripe grapes
their wine ... I declare to you, that for the time I lived as in
a musky meadow ... I felt divinely free from all ill-will, or petulance,
or malice... Squeeze! squeeze! squeeze! all the morning long;
I squeezed that sperm till I myself almost melted into it.
I squeezed that sperm till a strange sort of insanity came over me;
and I found myself unwittingly squeezing my co-labourers hands in it,
mistaking their hands for the gentle globules ... Come; let us
squeeze hands all round; nay, let us all squeeze ourselves into each other.'
And Melville loved every part of the whale - from the mighty head,
with the secret citadel of the brain, via hump, spout, epidermis,
blubber, bones, and bowels of fragrant ambergris, to the powerful
twin flukes of the man-killing tail. And, 'such an idol as that
found in the secret groves of Queen Maachah in Judea, and for
worshipping which, king Asa, her son, did depose her',
Leviathan's foreskin, the size of a man, and, given two armholes,
donned and worn as a 'cassock' by blasphemous men.

And what is the reward for this sumptuous masterpiece?
It sinks, like the Pequod, with barely a trace. Barely a cent
for impoverished Herman. While William gets rich
by extolling the virtues of voluntary poverty in
The Varieties of Religious Experience. These are the jokes
of the prankster God. And no redemption for Herman
in this unjust world. The sentence was life. Instead of writing
great novels, twenty years as a clerk in the Custom House,
the pen that created Leviathan put to calculating tax.

'A panharmonicum' - Emerson's term for the writing he sought,
like the organ combining all the sounds of an orchestra -
violins, clarinets, trumpets, trombones, flutes and a full range
of percussion instruments, triangles, cymbals and bass drums.
In such writing, 'everything is admissible - philosophy,
ethics, divinity, criticism, poetry, humor, fun, mimicry, anecdote -
all the breadth and versatility of the most liberal conversation,
highest and lowest ... all permitted and combined in one speech'.
But when Melville did exactly this with *Moby-Dick* the book
flopped - the unwonted always unwanted by an agoraphobic
public scared of the inordinacy of the ocean, and needing

the familiar compartments and categories. The *New York Globe*:
'The author has not given his effort here the benefit of knowing
whether it is history, autobiography, gazetteer, or fantasy'.

Melville, forgotten as a writer, gave up the country home
he could no longer afford and moved to New York City
and a life of anonymous servitude.

Always the city is the society of the solitary, the reward
of the failure, the sanctuary of the heretic, the asylum of the lunatic,
the sole habitat of the rare and endangered species, the garret seer,
who came down to the street to invent *flânerie*, the urban walk
whose only goal is to unify the two most sophisticated
superorganisms – human consciousness and the city.

The two first *flâneurs* – in the old world Baudelaire the despiser
who railed against commerce, and in the new world Whitman
the affirmer who revelled in the 'mettlesome, mad, extravagant city',
writing to his lover, a streetcar conductor, 'You know it is
a never ending amusement and study and recreation for me …
a sort of living, endless panorama – shops and splendid buildings
and great windows: and on the broad sidewalks crowds of women
richly dressed continually passing … men too dressed in high style,
and plenty of foreigners – and then in the streets the thick crowd
of carriages, stages, carts, hotel and private coaches, and in fact
all sorts of vehicles and many first class teams, mile after mile,
and the splendour of such a great street and so many tall,
ornamental, noble buildings many of them of white marble,
and the gayety and motion on every side: you will not wonder
how much attraction all this is on a fine day, to a great loafer
like me, who enjoys so much seeing the busy world move
by him, and exhibiting itself for his amusement,
while he just takes it easy and looks on and observes.'

WALT WHITMAN CLOSE says the street sign. I feel he is.
 Laughing behind curtains there, or disguised on the street
– the sullen overweight mother with the double pushchair
… who seems not to see or hear …the character proffering
leaflets with flames of hellfire (but a message I agree with:
No Salvation After Death), or the girl in school uniform

emerging from The Evelyn Grace Academy to shout
across the street gaily, 'Up your arse, wanker!'

No, Walt insisted we all must *become him*. So *I* am Walt Whitman,
of London the son, the pavement quest hero, metropolitan mystic,
a Pan-about-town, pluripotent, perfervid, a thaumaturge, demiurge,
maestro, magnifico, under a spell and hence over the top,
manic manic bipolar (up and then further up), creator, curator,
igniter, aerater, no frozen sixty-nine, limber and eager,
(running right up every Underground escalator,
even that incredibly long one in Holborn), a grey superhero,
the Incredible Husk, prizing all that is light and swift,
lithe and blithe, buoyant, agile, all that's learning and growing
and metamorphosing, flying right in the face of, and boldly
defying, gravity, inertia and petrifaction, on the winged sandals
of Perseus slaying the Gorgon who turns men to stone.

Reborn once more, I'm afoot with my vision in the great
diverging multiplicity still always one. Cheetah Cars,
Big Bite Kebab and Fried Chicken, Bumpa Selection
Mens Clothing, it is all one to me. Washing-draped
tower block and puddle-pocked underground car park,
thunderous flyover and urinous underpass, all one to me.

Camerados, I give you the hand of the Whitman of London.
Mix and become a new unity. Belong absolutely but circulate
freely. Urban pantheism is a non-stick pan. Come, I give you
my hand in sincerely cordial (but metaphorical)
meet and greet (it would utterly ruin my marvellous thoughts
if one of you would actually approach and speak).

Come with me now (metaphorically at least) past
The Go Sing Chinese Takeaway, Klassy Looks Hair and Beauty,
Majestical Lips (which seems to sell mainly men's caps),
Catwalk Wigs (Dr Miracle's Feel It Formula sold here),
The Kharisma Café, The Courtesan Dim Sum Bar, Uncle Ned's
Beds and The Light of God Celestial Church of Christ.
Then along to the Material Recycling Facility (bulkers only
by this gate) and the Mahatma Gandhi Industrial Estate.

For Walt was 'by thud of machinery and shrill steam-whistle
undismay'd, bluffed not a bit by drain-pipe, gasometers,
artificial fertilizers' - surely the only poetic celebrant of
artificial fertilizers, the only nineteenth-century man to predict
the multiverse, and characteristically unperturbed by even this
crazy idea, 'Let your soul stand cool and composed
before a million universes', unifying even such multitudes,
'And a song make I of the One form'd out of all'.

The great despisers loathed, and the great affirmers loved, trade,
by which every city is made. Whitman sold toothbrushes.
Thoreau sold pencils, which he also designed and manufactured.
Emerson approved: 'Henry Thoreau has made, as he thinks,
great improvements in the manufacture, and believes he makes
as good a pencil as the good English drawing pencil.
They are for sale at Miss Peabody's for 75 cents the dozen.'
Imagine Schopenhauer peddling toothbrushes door to door.
Flaubert or Baudelaire as a sales rep for pencils.

The esurient city becomes the new home. All roads lead to Rome.
Now is the time and right here is the place, advised Horace,
the canniest Roman, who threw away his sword and shield
and fled from the battlefield. Prophecy is only for charlatans
and idiots and no one can tell if we've decades of soul-forging
winters ahead or may not make it through to the next.
The trick is to accept and make use of what happens, be always
alert and sly, chill a white, open a red to breathe, and work overtime
to get over time, elude time by hiding within it, riding the tiger
by getting inside it. Eternity lives in the belly of time.

    So never anticipate and never regret.
    Look neither forward nor back but around.
    The more you expect the less you get.
    The less the lost the more the found.

      Right here is your heaven,
      Says every true prophet.
      Take what you're given
      And make something of it.

Time alters everything, even itself. The bare-assed Neanderthals
had shorter lives but more time. Once upon a time we had all
the time in the world. Now the longer we live the less time we have.
In our time it all happens in no time at all. How to deal
with this demiurge? Don't try to measure it, beat it or cheat it.
Escape time by ceasing to wish to escape it. I will not deny,
try to defeat, never fear, hate nor rage at, but humbly submit to time.
Let us pray once more: 'Creator, transformer, destroyer, renewer,
Lord of the Manifold Unity, Master of Microbe and Galaxy, God
of the River, hold me in close to the heart of the flux, bear me up
and sweep me along in the flow, carry me down to the bitter sea.'

Time is the implacable foe we must never kill but learn to love
and Eternity is the beautiful hope we must never love but learn to kill.
Time is the drum of Dionysus, leading the dance of the beauty
that passes – and Eternity is the petrified dream of Narcissus,
me forever and forever me.

It is certainly time to collect my little granddaughter, Mia,
latest triumph of the frolicsome dust, incarnate energy and interest.
Only the unworldly notice the world – so, both free, detached,
we're the perfectly matched masters, *Not Yet* and *No More*,
pausing every now and then to exchange deadpan koans.
'Mia, what is the meaning of life?' 'Allo.' Rolling ebulliently
through the streets, we throw our cries back at the vehement wind
and thank the Goddess of the world who has scattered garlands
in our path, a gravity-denying dog turd challenging heaven
with a ziggurat, and another two-tone, dark below
and green on top, a chocolate and pistachio double scoop,
then a cloud-reflecting, shining pool and a chestnut tree
that asperges us playfully as we pause, for even a scruffy tree base
can be magical if seen through the eyes of a young child.
In the stony square of soil around the rough, knobby trunk,
a swinging insouciant gypsy jazz of dark mosses, dandelions
(in bloom and sere), rough grass and grateful weeds enjoying asylum
from the salubrious suburbs' killing fields, and all this thrumming
with insect life, a manifold paradise that's attracted a snail,
whose trail across the pavement glitters in light returning now.
The Way shines and the destination burgeons and thrives.

Mia, show me the way from detachment to oneness,

compartments to wholeness, shrinking to growing, petrifaction
to flowing, and make me as panoptically conscious,
microscopically curious, as constantly eager to learn as you are.
'Infancy,' Emerson cried, 'is the perpetual Messiah,
which comes into the arms of fallen men, and pleads with them
to return to paradise.' Mia, teach me to heed always
the imperative of the organism. Everything alive
is obliged to strive, to learn, adapt, transform, emerge.

Learn to strive ... and strive to learn.
                Know
                To grow.
                Solve
                To evolve.
                Understand
                To command.
                Life is cognition
                So hit the ignition.
Seek out and suck in the energy to burn.

Life is such bountiful interdependence,
                Not overt and solid
                But covert and fluid,
                Symbiosis
                And osmosis,
                Low creepings,
                Deviant seepings,
                Intertwinings,
                Underminings,
All so gradual and secret there seems no emergence,

Only repetition, sameness, inertia and nullity,
                The burning of energy
                Bringing, not butterfly
                Metamorphosis,
                Morning-after halitosis,
                Total paralysis,
                Terminal stasis,
                The change imperceptible
                Till suddenly incredible.
Look at a mirror ... your children ... your city.

All at once the unpredictable new thing appears
        In a random mutation
        Or a quantum vibration,
        Popping a something
        Out of the nothing.
        Power shifts,
        A cloud lifts
        And you learn
        What you earn
Is old age, the free lunch you've been buying for years.

First, the device is hooded, conferring a conspiratorial *frisson*,
the dangerous exposure of the deep cover agent contacting control.
Then the decisive grip and swift ingestion of the card
have a confident authority that reassures. And congenial too
the laxity of these loose keys, so relaxed in their settings,
but yet with a solid integrity, like old-fashioned doorknobs,
suggesting a willingness to negotiate with, and adapt to, the finger
already comfortably ensconced in the concave indentation on top.
For good pressing there must be a continual development,
a changing sensation that leads, ineluctably, to final engagement.
Seeming not to resist, the key suddenly brakes, then abruptly
desists with a satisfying sense of conclusive internal enmeshing.
Children, natural phenomenologists, always love to press keys,
and this is a pleasure adults should treasure, for soon there may
only be touch screens, which offer no haven or purchase
for the wandering fingertip and lack the responsiveness of keys,
the interaction and accommodation, the stages of getting acquainted,
tentative foreplay, full engagement and consummation.
Pressing a metal key is a minuscule moment of consensual sex.
And it consummates with a wad of notes, pristine or laundered
cotton sheets as crisp as newly-starched shirts and as firmly aligned
as hospital sheets, but alive with potential … rebirth certificates
… letters of transit … promissory notes … angel wings.
Though this machine is reluctant to surrender its bounty.
It holds on, and offers the resistance that provides the perfect
end to the experience. For wresting a destiny from the clutch
of the gods invests it with agency, potential and power.
Give me my money, you scheming bank! *Hah!*

A rare experience of sensual repletion in a world of sensory deprivation,

that increasingly attempts to starve three of the senses. Lightweight
materials rob us of heft, background music makes us deaf, deodorants
deny us smell, and disdainful shiny surfaces refuse finger sex.
I want aural, olfactory and tactile acuity - a body of knowledge.
I want to get in touch with the whole thing, hear what it has to say,
sniff out its secrets, with the mind of a Hegel and the snout of a beagle,
think like a philosopher but sense like an animal, and put both
together to enrich the phenomenal, really get a grip on it,
following my nose but with an ear to the ground.

Viewers, voyeurs, visual gluttons, slavish votaries of the gaze,
there is more to the whole thing than meets the eye,
and there seem to be hints in the teasing wind.
Get on the scent of it, prick up your ears, feel your way.

But with what shall the doors of perception be oiled?
What will attune the arrays of receptors, not just to spot,
grab, devour, but to scrutinise, harken, sniff, fondle and savour?

Halted and humbled, I pause on the threshold, like a peasant
at the door of the Cathedral in Seville, overawed
by the sacred - the silence, the icons, the incense, the faithful.
When I think of how often words saved me, words fail me.
Wordless, I pray in my wordy cathedral, with its many secluded
side chapels devoted to poetry, philosophy, history, biography,
and a crypt for cosmology and microbiology, my icons
the photos of masters and my incense the scent of new volumes.
Books, books, on the shelves, on the trolleys, in the worshipful hands
of believers, and invitingly piled on wide tables for the predatory
senses to ogle, fondle, heft, riffle, flip and sniff … and possibly
bear off to hoard in a lair. This intoxicating incense
is a secondary emergence, the odours of paper, adhesive,
ink and boards combined in the fragrance of each book,
and then all the book bouquets combined in a body-and-soul
soothing fragrance, like that of the warm, sweet-smelling breaths
and silken, aromatic skins of the shining ones in paradise.

Heaven indeed, but the atmosphere of devotional finality is illusory.
As in the void, the solemn silence seethes with hidden energy and life.

A great book is a process not a thing, its ramifying energies
barely contained, irresponsible and irrepressible, and it probably
never developed in a straight line from top-down control
but in bottom-up accruing, mutating and merging that threatened to,
and frequently succeeded in, bursting the form. So, needless to say,
it refuses completion, and is tragically abandoned to publication
like a child handed over to the insensitive authorities,
but survives this catastrophe to continue surprising,
and becomes even more surprising over the years
as it exults in eluding the critical pursuers.

The cosmos, nature, human life - excess, excess and more excess,
which can never be grasped, but only sensed and humbly served
in excessive books, exuberant and exorbitant, madly
(and often also maddeningly) inordinate: *The Canterbury Tales*,
Gargantua and Pantagruel, *Don Quixote*, *Tristram Shandy*,
Leaves of Grass, *Moby-Dick*, *Zarathustra*, *Ulysses, In Search of Lost Time*.
For fuck's sake, Geoff, Francois, Miguel. For fuck's sake,
Laurence, Herman, Walt. And for fuck's sake, Friedrich, Jim, Marcel.

It is much too much for the much too little.
We are put here on earth to be overwhelmed.

Even the sentences excessive - at the same time torrential
and nonchalant, surging and circling, plunging and dawdling,
with windings, poolings, dams and falls, apparently random
but always directed, apparently lawless but always controlled.

Even the words, the atoms, excessive. Savour like fine wines,
say like the names of the Hindu deities, string like a necklace
of precious stones. Each week a word of the week, that was
last month *fructify*. Last week *trundle*. This week *fissiparous*.
Short list for next week - skulk, epiphenomena,
aerodrome, thurible, gusset and drool.

I would happily pay through the nose with my crackling, pristine
wad of notes but here there are new books, and big fragrant hardbacks,
at greatly reduced cost. Down in Remainders I seek truth and beauty

at half price or less … and immediately find, for just £3.99,
The Drunken Universe, a hefty anthology of Sufi poetry,
and then for £5.99 *The Soul of Rumi: A New Collection of Ecstatic Poems*
by Jelaluddin Rumi, and in a sumptuous American hardback edition.
Who could not love American books, as distinctive in form as in content
– the big, chunky print on the rich, creamy, rough-textured pages
with raggedy edges that open as readily as Whitman's shirts
to invite to their fragrant and generous breasts?
Two treasure chests of ecstasy – and change from a tenner.
In the nearest caravanserai, the bookshop's basement coffee shop,
I respect the Sufi reverence for unity by carefully prising up
and picking off the two cut-price stickers without causing
even the tiniest tear, and then, to enjoy Sufi energy,
(Rumi invented the dervish dance), use, as did Rumi, black coffee
to fire me up into dervish mode. 'Come out, come out!' Rumi cried,
'the masters are coming.' 'I'm not in the mood. I don't feel well today.'
'I don't care if you're *dead*. All the better in fact.
This is Jesus looking to *resurrect* someone.'

Connection! James on Sufi thinkers: 'The transport
attained by their methods is like an immediate perception,
as if one touched the objects with one's own hands.'

Connection! Emerson loved Sufi poets and especially Hafiz,
'at once tender and bold, with great arteries', who 'accosts all topics
with an easy audacity', loves 'the play of wit and the joy of song',
and desires only 'to give vent to his immense hilarity and sympathy'.
'Come, Saqi,' cried Hafiz, 'bring wine, for this Parthenon
of desire is set on unstable stones and the joists of life
are laid on the four vagrant winds'.

Connection! Emerson on Whitman: a combination of
'the Bhagavad Gita and the New York Tribune'.
Said with a touch of exasperation. But isn't it perfect?
Ancient truth in a contemporary megaphone.

Connection! Thoreau also loved eastern thought, and believed
that Whitman would too. 'Wonderfully like the Orientals,'
he said of Walt, and, after a visit to Walt in New York,

when asked if he had read these, Walt answered, 'no, tell me.'

And the quest is at last an equal opportunities employer.
From Kansas, Dorothy, the bravest quest heroine,
sets forth in search of the Great Oz in the Emerald City
at the end of the yellow brick road. With the scarecrow,
the tin man and the cowardly lion, she traverses dark forests,
deep ditches, a river, escaping the deadly poppies
and slaying the monstrous Kalidahs with heads like tigers
and bodies like bears, the forty eye-pecking crows,
forty wolves, killer bees and winged monkeys
and the Wicked Witch of the West. Here at last
is the palace of the Great and Terrible Oz. And the great
and terrible discovery – The Great Wizard is in fact a Great Fraud.
A little old man, wrinkled and bald. The throne a cheap prop,
The Great Head made of paper, the Mighty Voice a trick
of ventriloquism and the ball of fire a cotton wad.

Now the quest heroines are as weary, bewildered and frustrated as men
and just as powerless to quit. One ageing Dorothy, worn but undaunted,
puts up aching feet and scans the book on her knees with sapiental
keen eyes, while this other grunts and makes vehement margin notes,
putting a high gloss on dull text. And here comes a unity of gravity
and levity – a girl in a light dress lugging a heavy tome, *Birth and Beyond*.
To look upon mortal beauty is to stare at the eyeball-searing sun.
Yet the eye is irresistibly drawn. This is not lust ... though sex is in it
of course ... just the miracle of blossom as revealed to the husk.

Look down. In this little cup there is not just a double espresso
but a story of arrogant rational contempt and humble sensual return.
Mother's china tea sets were the symbols of gentility,
expensive, delicate, fussy, impractical. It was never even possible
to get a finger through the handle and grip the cup properly.
So, contemptuous, dismissive, I rejected cups for mugs.
Into the generous aperture I thrust a forefinger and waved,
brandished, *wielded* the mug. A mug could be a weapon
... and I mugged my own mother (symbolically at least).
Anger and aggression I now regret. It is time to atone
by reassessing mug and cup. To 'mug' is to assault but to 'cup'
is to cherish. The mug also represents the error of quantity,

the error of the overweight USA. Life is qualitative
not quantitative. There is more in a sip than a gulp
… more in a cup than a mug. More in an espresso than
an Americano. I would cup my cup … but I need forgiveness
from the tiny handle. To grip it tightly, with finger and thumb,
forces attention and concentration. And the saucer,
once despised as redundant, forces exactitude, and rewards
this with the satisfaction of unity restored, when the cup,
with a tinkle of pleasure, precisely touches down in its ring.
This is so fitting, the saucer sings. And the teaspoon,
dismissed as outdated and decorative – insulted by Eliot
as the symbol of decadence, yet has found a new vocation
as a measurer of medicine, spiciness and herbiness,
a dispenser of sweetness and headiness (a miniature wok
for cooking crack), a master of the crucial, transformative tinch,
the revelatory sip that outdoes the blind gulp, another preacher
of quality rather than quantity, always judicious
but never conspicuous, exemplar of less in the age of more,
the scrupulous steward of beginnings and endings.
How else to get the last froth from the cup?
What wonders it could offer up! From deep space,
to demonstrate the heft of the tiny, a teaspoon of neutron star
is ten million tons. From rich earth, to demonstrate the wealth
of the tiny, a teaspoon of soil has more microbes than people
on earth. And, to demonstrate the power of the tiny, a teaspoon
of toxic botulinum would kill every person on earth.
These are a few of the many singular affordances of the spoon.
Which also has just the right length, heft and balance for tapping.
I chime my glass, strike my cup, make a bass drum of the tabletop
… listen and wait for the teasing pinch … wait to be stirred.

And stirring indeed is this arrival, with the burning conviction
of Rabi'a, the female Sufi saint who roamed through Basra's streets
with a bucket of water in one hand to put out hell's flames
and in the other a blazing brand to set fire to paradise,
crying out: 'Fear of punishment and hope of reward
have blinded us to the radiant visage of God.'
This new brigand buys cheaper coffee to go, and then,
openly, *brazenly*, sits down to drink it *here*, aggressively
crunching crisps (also bought elsewhere), defiantly shaking
and crackling the bag, and using crisps to register insolence,
as did chewing gum once, but with loud sound effects
for the age of noise. The bag is metallic, shiny, garish

and twice as big as it needs to be, like 50s American automobiles,
to encourage the crackling of packaging that amplifies
the fuck-*you* of crunching the product, the pleasure aural
as much as oral, with the antic crackle of a pile of lit twigs.
Covertly I watch as abruptly she puts bag aside now
to whip out a highlighter and, avidly biting off the top,
lifts and poises the tip. Here comes the day's major highlight,
I feel, as in a single, unfaltering stroke, bold and sure, she sweeps
right across the black print a broad swathe of bright blue.
It's the confident barbarism of her violation that excites me,
and Oh to know her major truth … or to join the quest
with any of these plucky Dorothys. May *I* be your
raggedy scarecrow, cowardly lion, tin man?
(Mother always accused me of 'acting the tin man'.)

And this unisex toilet has a feminine fragrance – or is it
just my imagination? It is certainly not the place for the rank
rebelliousness of piss. Often it demands to be released
and then refuses to start. Or the jet turns back in,
aiming for the trouser leg, or spurts out to one side,
deliberately, wilfully, missing the bowl. Or it cunningly
bifurcates exactly enough so the two jets can't fit in at once.
Or decides that today it's a sprinkler. Or a combo jet
and sprinkle (or jet and dribble). Especially provocative
and impertinent today, it shows off by bifurcating
into two jets that actually cross and shoot
in opposite directions. And then at the end it plays dead,
but waits till you're zipped up to let out a last gush,
proving the truth of that old Irish apothegm:

> *No matter how much you shake your peg,*
> *There's always a drop runs down your leg.*

The street tough who shat himself taught me that rhyme,
laughingly shaking and stowing his cock after peeing on flowers
in the Lucky Lane. I saw him again, over fifty years later,
on a rare visit home, when he passed on the street,
his red roughened face ravaged by years, abuse, anger
and discontentment, his body heavy, hair greying and thin.
Yet I knew him immediately, such is the power of memory

to extrapolate and match. But memory failed to produce a name.
He passed without seeing me. Should I have spoken? Excuse me,
we haven't met in more than half a century but you may have
inspired my career as a poet and the last time we met you had just
shat yourself. But I can't for the life of me recall your name?
This is the kind of opportunity you can only have by going home.

But at last, and by chance, his old staff, that could find little purchase
in Irish mud or desert sand, discovers firm ground, and the earth
resonates to its resonant thump. He becomes as one possessed
by authority. Like a priest in the temple, he stands by
an electronic altar and at the touch of a button a great screen
descends with a measured thunder. With another touch he calls
from the high ceiling light to shine forth in the darkness
and illuminate the screen, and in his right hand raises high
his seeker's staff, his sword of truth – a wireless mouse.
Employed to explain Information Systems, he tells them of what
he has come to believe, that everything is relation and process,
that everything flows, as Heraclitus proposed (though it only
pays to study data and especially cash flows). That everything
in a system is connected, and so changing one thing will change
all the others, producing unpredictable side effects,
which is what baffled managers never accept. They believe
they can change only one thing and keep all the rest.
And the regular failures of computer systems are rarely
the consequence of technical problems but due to embedding
in human systems. The problem, my friends, is not in the wires
but in ourselves - that we are all contrary and hate change,
or, rather, we hate change imposed from above,
and will subvert and sabotage. System users will fold arms
like Bartleby and say, I prefer not. Therefore systems must start
with the users and grow bottom-up from what users want
   … but of course human users never know what they want,
so development must go in circles of build a bit, try it,
acknowledge mistakes and revise. Just like the messy,
contrary users, IT systems must *evolve*. So bottom-up
and around and around is always the way for these systems
to grow. Respect the invisible network connections. Nodes always
believe that they're running the show - but it's really the flow.

Ants are dumb but their systems are smart, he explains,

whereas humans are smart but their systems are dumb.
Command and control can't react and adapt fast enough
so the problems cascade and top down goes tits up.
For the managers fail to understand that their systems
are shackled by chains of command, and that this is
the Age of Morphogenesis, when arthritic old hierarchies
creak and ache, and limber networks morph and segue
… when bottom-up once again complements top-down.
For top-down is blind and rarely sees bottom-up
but bottom-up is always well aware of top-down,
and will cunningly, ingeniously undermine.

It is always the hierarchy versus the network, top-down
versus bottom-up, central control versus self-organising.
Which one should triumph? Neither must triumph.
Let them cohabit in fruitful tension.

So at last, from the turbulence of bottom up meeting
top down, democracy, not an eternal ideal all must find,
but a human invention of place and time, emerges gradually,
uncertain and vulnerable, never the philosopher king
grandly wise, but fractious, timid, indecisive,
stumbling round the same cycle of crisis and bargaining,
makeshift expediency and ramshackle compromise,
with little idea of where it is blundering, committing mistakes
and correcting them, veering left then right, inching forward,
pulling back, ignoring threats, missing opportunities,
hearing only the most numerous who shout loudest and longest,
its event horizon the next election, always bewildered,
frustrated, exhausted, and always tempted to return
to the purity of personal vision and the simplicity of strength.

Nor is democracy about equality. Who wants equality?
Democracy is the freedom for all to feel superior in their own way.
(So, nowadays a passionate democrat, I feel myself
immensely superior for having had such an original thought).

But exhausted democracy yearns for simplicity, and desires
to become administration, to sit in a comfortable office

and manage day-to-day routine. So democracy petrifies
into bureaucracy, and the hierarchy takes on a life
of its own to become a strange new God, the State.

Now the quest hero has no name but K, and just wants
to get into the Castle to start on the task he has been engaged
to complete, and for which, by an arduous journey, he has
come a long way. Yet even this modest grail is hard to attain.
To begin with, this hero's no longer heroic but just a surveyor,
a measurer, armed with a tape not a sword, and the tests
are more complex, the foes more formidable, subtle
and devious, invisible administrators, the inscrutable hierarchy.
K arrives and sets off through the village but the way is deep
in snow and just seems endlessly to circle the Castle,
which is not the imposing stronghold its name would suggest,
but a rambling huddle of little houses with crumbling plaster.
Eventually it grows dark and K, cold and weary, turns back
to the village inn with its taciturn customers and bad-tempered
landlady, as, from the Castle, comes the sound of a bell, mingling
promise and menace, the threat of fulfilling some unknown desire.
Then Frieda, the barmaid with a superior manner,
drags K to the floor underneath a bar counter where they roll
in a litter of food scraps and pools of spilled beer. Instead of
moving with the prudence befitting his ambition and the power
of the adversary, K has wallowed in garbage and incurred
the obligation to marry a barmaid. And is he even engaged
by the Castle? It seems the instruction was issued some time ago
and sent in error to the wrong department. Now no one is sure
if his services are still required. A courteous letter
from a Castle official appears to confirm the appointment
but the Superintendent in the village, K's immediate superior,
while also courteous, rejects this interpretation. K is not from
the Castle or the village, and is not wanted, really just
a troublesome stranger who should leave and return
whence he came. But when K remains, the Superintendent,
generous and courteous, offers, as a great favour,
the temporary and provisional post of school janitor.

Desiring never to hold a high office but only to sit in a high office,
sipping black coffee, the quest hero brings out the serious
and responsible black-handled scissors that enclose and conceal

their sharp edge, are not for mad brandishing, no stabbing,
slicing or chopping - or even fist grabbing - but insist on
being carefully taken up with carefully separated fingers
and thumb. Only when assured of a fastidious user
will the sharp blades appear. Tool of the artisan
not the barbarian, tool of tailor, barber and surgeon,
an existential philosopher that trims off the clutter,
chooses a line and crisply, cleanly, follows through,
conferring for a moment, on a slovenly life, direction,
decisiveness, exactitude and grace. Rapt, he snips out
the useful bits from the photocopied pages of textbooks,
affixes them to a blank page with Pritt Stick and brushes out
the photocopy smears with Tippex, so that this will appear
to be an original handout when it is photocopied again.
High in his office, high on black coffee and high on
the intoxication of forgery and the heady scent of
forger's tools, Pritt Stick and Tippex, he looks benignly down
on the quad with its swarmings of students and single tree,
and his troubled heart is now at peace - the old copy monk
Philophylus, he who dwells with and learns from the leaves
- that brief is the blossoming, brief the bloom,
and brief the dance of lustres in the zephyrs of summer.

Nothing seems to be changing - and yet all has changed.
The self is completely transformed though it feels just the same.
Somehow it has all gone from hard to soft, cold to warm,
static to dancing, solid to fluid, certain to doubtful,
analytic to heuristical, optimal to possible, linear to circular,
cerebral to physical, abstract to concrete, thusness to thisness,
timeless to timebound, know-all to know-nothing, separate to unified,
parts to whole. From the righteous God to the merciful Goddess.
From the European despisers to the American affirmers.
From the stag on the crag to the doe in the flow.
From the need to control to the need to let go.

It is time now to put away his warped old bow,
and his learned books, compass and charts. Still keen the eye,
the barbs as sharp, the aim as true - but he has lost the will
to seek and shoot. Now at day's end he sits by the Heraclitus River,
in thrall to the winding and shining, the music and flow,
at once replete and yearning, melancholy and blithe,

by the mystery of time both enriched and deprived,
and by and by cuts a reed from the bed by the bank
and fashions a mouthpiece and four finger holes.
In the mercy of harsh light that ripens to glow,
with a flute from the river he'll compass the world.

Acknowledging the limits of personal agency, he yields with good grace to contingency, the necessary and random in harmonious tandem.

Acknowledging his impotence in the tyranny of time, he is reconciled to process and the sovereignty of dust.

Acknowledging as toxins disgust and contempt, he agrees to praise the whole thing (though golf and celebrity chefs are exempt).

Acknowledging that detachment is impossible, as is any truth objective and permanent, he consents to enigmatic entanglement.

Acknowledging the lack of a definitive User Guide, he makes do with dubious defaults, coarsely-grained filters and provisional heuristics.

Acknowledging the ongoing shortage of Masters, and the ongoing whitening and thinning of hair, he designates himself as his own aged Master.

And is troubled anew by a realisation - that maybe the Grail
was the Goddess with loins on fire. That after all not Galahad
but Sir Bors and Percevale found the Grail, that maybe
the Grail sought the hero and the fool spurned the Grail
to go seeking the Grail. Doesn't this sound like one of God's
elegant jests? Would a Goddess return? Can the fire in
the loins be rekindled? A love dead so long be reborn?
No birth more difficult. All that was thrown away in an instant
can take forty years to win back. For all that is good is hard
to acquire and easy to lose - exactly the opposite of all that is bad.
This new love is no lightning bolt, just a slow, imperceptible regrowth
that needs constant tending. Love is not rapture but diligence.
So work to love and love to work. Work for the symbiotic union
when the two become one. A lover's work is never done.

Love may yearn for equilibrium, the reward of repose – but equilibrium is death, disequilibrium is life.

Love does not like holding hands on the sofa but needs to be just about to go supernova.

Love, like life, thrives on the border with chaos, on the brink of breakdown and disorder.

Love is explosive symbiosis, the fusion always verging on fission, a turmoil of strong, contradictory urges.

Love is a bond of dark energy in the greater dark energy, a fizzing force field in the greater force field.

Love is a chaotic system, sensitive to minuscule changes in input (one innocuous word and all hell can break loose).

Love, like particle and wave, flips between opposing states - to surrender and dominate, wound and be wounded, worship and hate.

Love is a wrestling which may be more thrilling to lose than to win. To throw − yes, exciting - but lord to be suddenly, heavily *thrown*.

Love is symbiosis, but a symbiotic autonomy - only those who can be alone can be successful together.

Love passeth all understanding and logic. What equations could capture the turbulence of the magma chamber of the human heart?

Love does not care to be understood, and even less to be dismissed out of hand. Love dumps you and not the other way round.

Love loves to grab the proud one at the high window, rip off the priestly robes, roll naked flesh in the gutter, make it grovel and whimper.

Love is imperious, wilful, unreasonable, and demands the impossible, over and over, repeats, like young children and publishers, *do that again*.

Somehow love must foil inertia and defy gravity,
Make two heavy, ageing bodies take off and fly,
    Then get up from bad crash landings

And with more mock mockery, genuine flattery, drollery,
Coy innuendo and straight dirty talk - perpetual foreplay -
    Forge once more in secret secret wings.

Now let the singers go before and after them the players on instruments,
and the damsels on timbrels, for the great rupture, so long a sorrow,
is healed, as dispassionate science and the passionate Goddess
are reconciled. Concedes Science: 'I need your warm heart.'
Sighs the Goddess: 'I need your cool head.' Now Science has learned
how to touch, Goddess how to detach. Now Science has learned
how to wonder, the Goddess to ponder. Now Science loves
hot smelly creatures and the Goddess cool abstract ideas,
and when these two conjoin in the unity, and dance in the process,
and the dual organism has a dual orgasm, then not only the earth
… but the *universe* … no, the *multiverse* … moves.

And science, convinced it had everything measured and mastered,
has its confidence suddenly shattered. From the depths
of apparently empty space to the heart of apparently
passive matter, all is revealed as unknowable, manic.
There is no cosmic clock or universal container. Time and space
are a web of connection, time is process and space is relation,
and matter is simultaneously particle and wave, can be always
in more than one place, pass through apparently impermeable walls,
or may not even exist at all, and behaves entirely randomly,
but it is never possible to measure more than half of what goes on
and what is observed is dependent on who is observing,
and how and why. We see things not as they are but as *we* are.

Matter only *seems* solid, space only *seems* void, the nothing
is something, the something is nothing, and God cackles:
Which is more wacko, the micro or macro? As the cosmos
expands and contracts, out and back, out and back,
His majestic melodeon … playing a jig … and His
minuscule fiddle's the vibrating strings at the heart of the quark.
God's a chancer, a prankster, a fiddler, who plays not just dice
but perverse tricks and wild gypsy music. Let's dance.

Science, incredulous, sees demolished its pillars
– Objectivity, Certainty, Causality, Consistency and Finality.
And the century of little faith discovers the price of the freedom
it craved, and by the River of Heraclitus sits down to lament.

> So now we must make do by making do,
> With no fixed point from which to view,
> No sure beliefs to steer us through,
> No final truth to journey to.

The riches of youth are convictions … and the riches of age
are contradictions. Therefore never more accepting but never
more sceptical, never more worshipful but never more irreverent,
never more desolate but never more nonchalant, never more
detached but never quicker to weep, never more interested
in so much but never more aware that it all means so little,
never so certain that everything matters because nothing

matters, and that nothing is more serious than comedy
because nothing is more comical than seriousness.

Master Tseng and Master Yü walk with Novice Chien Wu by the river at evening.

'Master Tseng,' enquires Chien Wu, 'what is Way?'

Master Tseng: 'Asked what is Way, the Master said *walk on.*'

'But what is the destination?'

Master Yü answers, 'Way is higher than Heaven and yet not divine, beneath the six levels and yet never deep, preceding antiquity and yet not old, greatest of all things and yet not a thing, truer than knowledge and yet not a truth, stronger than sovereign decree and yet urging no action, incessantly journeying yet never arriving. There is a Way but no destination.'

Master Tseng has turned to the water: 'The gleam of the river at twilight.'

Master Yü turns to the trees. 'The wild monkey shriek in the forest.'

And Master Yü, after a sharp glance at Master Tseng, speaks thus to Chien Wu: 'The true school has only one Master and only one Novice.'

'Yes,' agrees Master Tseng: 'And both the same person.'

'The easy thing,' Master Yü resumes, addressing Tseng, 'is to become a Master. 'The difficult thing is to become a Novice.'

Novice Chien Wu looks from one to the other, 'Masters, what is unity in process?'

Master Tseng stops and plants his staff on the river bank. 'Why do the fireflies flash together?'

Master Yü raps his staff seven times on the ground: 'Because crickets chorus as one.'

Master Tseng turns to the novice. 'That which we know must be said is forever unsayable. There is a Destination but no Way.'

Now Novice Chien Wu startles the Masters by suddenly throwing his staff in the river, where its splash makes the fireflies go dark and the crickets fall mute.

'There *is* a Destination *and* a Way,' cries Chien Wu. 'The Destination is Chu Po Yu's wine shop and the Way is by this forest path.'

And the timorous Irish quest hero finally makes it to the USA
(where he should have gone with Stewart many decades before).
And a contemporary American Master, another affirmer,
though old and withdrawn to a small town, agrees to a visit.
The quest hero makes the long journey, descends from the train
… to a car park with long rows of automobiles – but no people.
Behind are white houses whose decks fly the flag
and whose yards have white tables with coloured umbrellas.

A sign: *We Support Our Troops. Please Come Home Safe.*
Platform poster: *I Love You, You're Perfect, Now Change
- the Hilarious Long-Running Hit Musical*. Silence and sultry
summer heat. No sign of life, much less the zest of a Master.
And this Master also explained that the quest and its journeys
are futile. His quest hero learns, from a mysterious lady,
of a place called Avalon, 'where you can walk',
and sets out to find it but fails, drives around and around
(the American quest is by automobile) and arrives, finally,
at the sea. When he contacts the lady she tells him he has
been clever because: 'Nothing is more beautiful than the sea'.

But the sea is out of sight on the far side of town.
And few sights are less beautiful than a shadeless car park
under fierce midday sun. Rows of vehicles, neatly-lined,
glitter and burn. Even to touch one would scorch skin.
As Li Po explained long ago, the Master will never show.
But this is America. Here he comes … in a checked shirt,
soiled pants and a worn baseball cap, apologetic, scurrying,
more like a janitor than master or mentor. This is America.
And the home not a hut but a huge house: 'I rarely have
visitors … but I think there's some Dewar's. *Ice?*'
The dreaded whiskey – but he would drink even hemlock
on ice for the Master's words. Ah but the Master is ill.
'I had cancer … it cleared … then came back. I feel fine
but it's these endless hospital visits. They're specialists, oh yes
… in checking your wallet's health. To the money counter first
… *every time*.' He drinks Dewar's grimly. 'And these yachts
like battleships. They sail up and down, back and forth,
out there,' a gesture towards the distant sea, 'and then drop anchor
… in order to do *what*?' The quest hero's first test. He fails,
miserably. The Master leans forward to shout, '*Watch TV.*'

But a second chance is granted. 'So what have you noticed
about our strange country?' And he sits back, scrutinising.
'Everything's bigger … even the toilet bowls.' The Master
laughs – but swiftly is grim once again. 'It's all size
and money in this country. *Status*. I loved my mad
old friend … yes, *him* … but at this awards thing he arrived
with that woman who makes reputations … yes, *her*
… and *stuck tight*. When she eventually left I went over

to joke. *Prizes*! *Critics*! No go. Not a smile. A stuffed turkey.
And his manager wife glaring at me. A bad influence.'
He chuckles, drinks. 'But this thing. I *need* …' Rises, leaves.
Three walls of books summon the quest hero. Emily of course.
And Elizabeth, *ah*. Connection. Connection. Network indeed
– but with these women. Then, on a little side table,
The Winged Energy of Delight … translations of Basho,
Rumi, Hafiz. Connection, connection, connection.
Over on the desk a stack of sheets. The final affirmation
of the Master … poems of praise, Sutras of Enlightenment.
A peek! No, he's coming back down the hall, jubilant, waving
the cap. 'Thank God for America's big bowls. I didn't miss.'

The Master walks the quest hero back to the station and they stroll across a sunlit common. The quest hero feels that he has died and gone to heaven, borne up aloft on the winged energy of delight.

So now he is strolling with Whitman in the gardens of paradise.

'There's the tree seat in your poem,' he cries.

'You're remarkably familiar with my work.'

'I've loved it all my life. Authentic vision is so rare.'

'What is my vision?'

Ah!

That the major events, the adventures, the journeys, the stormy relationships, are not as important as they seem.

Whatever we do and wherever we go, we end up in some ordinary place, hearing the creaking of beams in a ceiling, the cry of a bird in a wood, a susurrus of tyres on a road.

And the memories that linger are not of the major events but of a child's balloon careering across a deserted swimming pool, a patch of torn poster on a crumbling wall, the big silver spoons in a fancy hotel.

'These things make an unforgettable impression, as though there is a reason for being here, in one place rather than another.'

There must be a reason, and so we seek. But there is no reason, no Avalon. 'There is only earth: in winter laden with snow, in summer covered with leaves'.

Marvel not at the monuments of stone, you idolaters of substance,
but convert to the true faith and venerate process,
the mystery, music and dance of what passes …
the play of tree shadow, the sighing of leaves,
and the fugitive fragrance of bloom on the wind.
There is only the momentary exaltation at the momentary lustres

of the turning world. Therefore go with the dart of the current,
the swirl of the vortex, the thrash of the whitetop,
the play of the spray on the welter of water.
Only what passes is precious - the flash of the river not the gem.

All turmoil, chaos. Any poise is just pose. It is not that
the centre cannot hold - but that no centre ever was.
Not that meaning is gone - but never was.
Not that personal identity has been lost - but never was.
Not that all the solid melts in air - but never was.
No things but events. There is only occurrence.
And never a terminus. Nothing resolved.
Just the flow of the sacred days we largely profane,
deaf and blind in a hubbub and dazzle of flowing.
Liquid our lives and loves, liquid our world and selves
- and liquid my bracing, propitiatory rites,
in the morning the blessing of bitter black coffee,
and at evening the tart absolution of wine.

So artificial intelligence finally got smart when it learned
that it's dumb to think you know what you're doing,
but intelligent to feel your way like nature in the dark,
guessing badly, guessing better, lurching one way, then the other.

Soon now, say AI believers, smart machines will take over.
But even the machines find it difficult to cope.
I loaded my laptop so heavily, packing in more and more,
that finally it suffered a double hernia. Game but vain
its struggle to absorb and retain, while keeping abreast
of the new and remaining consistent, forwardly flexible
but backwardly compatible … and, like its owner,
getting slower to locate, retrieve, load. Increasingly,
it needed to pause for help … *Configuring Updates*.
But even so came blackouts - and like everything it died.

Come, seeker, fare forth once again, for this curious world
demands curious minds and the conundrum of the universe
awaits your solution. And whether random efflorescence
or divine intervention, the mystery is equally compelling

and the primary commandment is pay attention, though not
with a single-sense focus but an all-sense receptiveness,
not with the tense concentration of adults but the relaxed awe
of the child. For paying attention is never expenditure always
investment – and interest is frequently repaid with interest.

Therefore learn to see *now* as we see when we look back at *then*,
see in the present the beauty and glory that time will reveal,
the value of living disclosed to the dying, the radiant everyday
as it looks from the brink of eternal black.

Here, for instance, in the heart of the tumult, the city
has set up a still life on a rubbish bin as carefully as
Cézanne with his apples in a studio. Thus reborn in oneness
are a *Freshbe Sex On The Beach Sparkling Soft Drink* bottle,
two nested pieces of orange peel, yesterday's free evening paper
(displaying a headline, *Man 86 Takes Wife's Ashes On Skydive*)
and one limp, bedraggled, badly-stained woollen glove,
symbolising the inadequacy of human control.

Or the unity and harmony of the black youth in earphones
propelling a clothes rack on wheels, and pausing now to boogy,
even getting on down right in the middle of the street,
so the chorus line of designer dresses, only slightly hampered
by protective bags, in elegant unison coolly swing.
Or the play of the multiple reflections on the multiple surfaces
of multiple objects, many in motion. Take what you find
and cavort in it. Light has as much fun here on the street
as it does on the sea and now prefers, as is its right
in the democracy of things, the ontological sincerity
of a bent lager can to the pomp of this equestrian statue
whose mighty plinth the shining can derides and undermines.

A privilege to walk in the clemency of late light, when sun comes
down low, to our level, and wants not to burn but to burnish
the gables and chimneys of shabby doomed buildings,
the imminence of loss charging everything with beauty.

Like this noble old mansion block, a citadel of secrecy
in the open-plan city, foursquare, solid, sombre, tall,
with massive walls and heavy doors, on each corner a turret,
higher and more pure than even a garret. Once more
the temptation – to live up there … in Montaigne's tower
… a cell consecrated to the solitary raptures of thinking,
writing, reading, and watching French films in the evening,
but visited weekly by a sophisticated lover who also
has her own place and would never stay over …
a cell with a window high and wide to look down on
the trammels and toils of the world. But then I see
old Larkin up at the window, rancorous, desolate
and bleary, opening the morning bottle of sherry,
the petrified voyeur who tried to protect
himself from life to have more time to write
and succeeded so well he had no more to say.

'If I do not live with people, then with whom shall I live?' Kong Qiu asks
Lao Tzu. 'He who seeks only to perfume his own mind destroys the essential
relations.'

'You would know people only to judge them.'

'I would know people only to understand them. And to awaken them with
classics and *The Book of Odes*.'

'What are books? Only the Masters' footprints in the dust. And what are
words? Always and only late guests of the world, who must never be allowed to
behave as though the dwelling place is theirs.'

'Men have no insight and swiftly years pass. I would know men to teach
them of duty.'

'All this teaching and preaching,' Lao Tzu objects. 'Talk of duty and virtue
just irritates people. Duty must come from within as an impulse and not from
without as an edict. If you do not already have it within, you can never receive it
from without.'

Kong, straight-faced, looks to the South Mountains. 'And is this not
teaching … even preaching?'

Lao Tzu turns towards the sky in the North. 'Better by far to study Way –
how the heavens and earth assumed their courses, how the sun, moon and
scintillant stars came by radiance, how the trees and the plants know to bloom and
the birds and the beasts to flock and the fish in the oceans to flash in shoals.

Then you too shall learn to be guided by Way. Does the swan need to bathe
every day to stay white?'

But this most dispiriting time of day, late afternoon,
corresponds to life's bleakest time, late middle age.
Is it the sense of a lack of achievement in the day or the life?
Or just the long punishing hours and years? Spirits soar
but bodies tire. Enough walking for one day.
Carry me taddy like you done through the fair.
It is time to go home on a seat on a train.

Across from the platform, above the line, right at the top
of a building, a huge fluorescent graffito inscrutably catches
the last of the light. Someone must have risked life to cross
the electrified line, scale a thirty-foot wall and spray,
suspended, in the dark, or somehow descended a sloping roof
to hang over the edge and create, in the dark, upside down,
a high art combining the skills of Picasso and Spiderman.
All for the life-giving sun of attention – what everyone
wants to receive … but not give. For no one here marvels
… or even looks up, poking moodily with thumbs
at the screens of smart phones. (Eventually human thumbs
may evolve to be as dazzlingly nimble and fleet
as Brazilian footballers' feet.) Every time and place yearns
for an aid to confer occult power on the grasping right hand
and the phone is our contemporary magic prosthesis,
the ring of Gyges, the rod of Asclepius, the lamp of Aladdin,
though instead of rubbing vigorously on a lamp, it's enough to
touch lightly a lit screen to summon the genie and issue commands.
Genie, show me my messages, many and varied: I must be
important, a centre, a hub. Then show all my fun wealth in photos
and film clips of arms around shoulders, and beaming heads
leaning together: I must be great company, fun2bwith.

That very word *underground*. The very word *network*.
The very word *tunnel*. The underground resistance.
The network of agents. The tunnel to freedom.
And the map that is the passport of the city state of London,
the identity card of the cosmopolitan, the freed slave's papers
of manumission. Designed by an engineering draughtsman,
Harry Beck, (in his spare time, in 1931) it was dismissed
out of hand by his boss Frank Pick, (a typical manager,
who initially rejected an innovative idea but, as soon as a trial
indicated popularity, used it to sell the Underground and himself).

Beck's genius was to understand that how it all links up
is just as, and frequently much more, important than what
and where it all is. 'Connections are the thing', was the Eureka cry
of Harry as, rejecting any slavish conformity to geography,
he began with the bold simplicity of a rectilinear grid in black,
then Matissed it with primary colours and curves,
to give vibrancy, allure, rhythm, teach it to dance.
Once more I open the folded card, observe the bright grid
pulse and glow, and relish names on white nodes.
Those mythopoeic destinations – Chalfont & Latimer,
Roding Valley, Gallions Reach, Arnos Grove.
My occidental ideogram, rational talisman.
The treasure is the map itself and not the illusory buried gold.

Even the travellers seem to be different … intriguing, mysterious.
This is the freedom of the city – to be an enigma among the enigmas
in the radical rebellion of refusing to be known, and remaining
a mystery even to one's self, defying every classification.
Here few are defined by profession and none wear the uniforms
of established religion. No habit or niqab, hat or collar.
This is the underground, the realm of the secular,
the personal freedom break, the solitary quest in the dark unknown,
where the train thunders out of the tunnel to scream,
I'm the Argo, the fleet steed of Galahad, the yellow brick road.

But now it is rush hour, when the many standing crushed together
are not mysterious or intriguing but homeward-bound workers
ignoring each other, eyes unfocused, glazed, in air fetid
with tiredness, vexation and sweat – the happy hour cocktail
of working days. Where this evening are the unbroken seekers,
the Jasons pursuing a Golden Fleece, the Galahads hunting a Holy Grail,
the Dorothys in search of a wizard and awaiting the announcement:
Next stop Emerald City. Alight for ensorcellment, marvels and mystery?
Ah, there she is, sitting far down in the carriage – well over thirty
but not disillusioned, dark eyes still on fire with the flash
of intelligence and glitter of mischief, but beautifully veiled
in warm adult compassion. No gadgets, no headphones, absorbed
in a book. And a black Penguin classic, more disturbingly erotic
than a black basque and stockings. I'm practically fainting
in fascination, all my thirty-five trillion cells throb with rejoicing.
Even my teeth fillings thrill and sing. But what's the book title?

I strain towards the title. And abruptly she looks up ... *rises*
... *approaches* ... now with *a smile of recognition*.
Must be a student whose face I've forgotten.
But who could forget such a woman? This must be Alzheimer's
... terror ... *terror*. Still coming closer ... the smile
even warmer ... but turning to indicate the vacated position.
She is offering her seat to *an old man*.
Sweet Mother of God.

Balder, whiter ... none the wiser. Hintings, teasings, fleeting thoughts
that shy from capture, random memories, shifting moods,
the changing weather of the day in the gradual climate change of age.
It's a passage from certainty to mystery, with even the past
unpredictable, even the past now a shapeshifter, even the past
on the move. Youth ... maybe more sweet to recall than to live.
The impotent rages, vicious hatreds, black despairs and burning shames.
And maybe Stewart was right that my gift is to mock.
But somewhere I lost the urge to scourge. So it is that
I regard with equanimity the prospering charlatans, and with zealots
of banality walk undismayed. No more anger ... but neither serenity
... just incredulity on the short walk home. So this is what it comes to
... *this* ... the stunningly brazen indifference of the world
... and it demands not just to be accepted but *admired*.
It will end soon ... and badly. First forgetting ... then forgotten.
Write your name in water. Cast your song upon the wind.

Sanctuary, sanctuary for the aged one. In the sanctum sanctorum,
elysium, lair, cavern, temple, scriptorium - *home*. And the unity
that reassures sublimely reinforced when the orange-juice carton fits,
exactly and snugly, in the space on the shelf of the refrigerator door.

Like our children grown taller on the bounty of fridges, the fridges
themselves have grown taller and bulkier (American models
the biggest of course) and frequently now tower above us,
gleaming behemoths, each with the thick, heavy door of a bank vault,
but opening on a supermarket, brilliantly illuminated, cool and fresh,
with transparent compartments, drawers and shelves, and separate
areas for wine, milk, fruit and veg. And as in the supermarket,
the immaculate shining white surface denies time, corruption
and death, both of food and repository, and then by association

all those the two serve, assured that they will live and thrive
for ever when they look upon such varied and nutritious
food reserves – the vault and the supermarket meeting the need
to have cake and eat it, binge and hoard. Always reserves
encourage greed. Barely enough may be glad of enough
but plenty always wants more. Like banks, the fridge-freezers
are cold, shining, monumental, secretive, discreetly growing
and acquiring control. Already these food vaults are larger
and fuller and soon will be smarter, telling us what we need
before we even know ourselves. This one's intelligent,
sleek, self-assured … and yet … now and then …
at unpredictable times, the apparently superior machine
issues near-human sounds, plangent, low, long-drawn-out,
as eerie and equivocal as the cries of a fox on a city street at night.

And here is the reward for the eventful quest – a symbiotic union
of life and matter, thing and creature, ass and chair.
But the chair must be straight-backed, high and hard,
and there must be a second, higher chair for the feet.
In youth support the lower class, in age support the lower back.
In hot-blooded youth elevate the mind,
but in cold-blooded age elevate the feet.

In the solitude of a silent room space grows, time slows,
and both unify in a single experience. Home is
where the continuum of spacetime is revealed.
Merge and make the holy trinity of spacetimeself.

A nice little mature nap? An earned treat. *No.*
What needs to be done for the beloved's return?
New washer in the dripping tap. And …
What was that name? Still vivid the shit on his bare thigh
and vivid his face. But the name, the *name*.
Brush the front path and put on a dark wash.
Maybe just close the eyes for a second. No.
NO. Ah … a definite outline – four syllables,
starts with an M. A Mac name. *Mac* Something.
Reply to McCandless? Not now. Sounding interested
might start it up again. Even encourage him to visit London.
Just briefly close eyes. But never to sleep. Why is drowsing

so arousing? As the head goes down the cock comes up.
McGettigan? No. McLenihan? *No.* But close ... *very close.*

As is sharpening pencils to writing, and grinding of beans
to coffee making, so is chopping to cooking – a serene
preparation rite. In a good knife the handle and blade
should have equal weight, blade springy, bright, with the strength
and intelligence to know when to bend, and the knife in the hand
should have meaningful heft, just a hint of the reassuring heft
of the sword. I grasp and heft with gratitude this heavy knife,
feeling strong in its wielding and sharp in its edge ...
also radiant and pliable, ready now to cut through
all hindrances to awakening i.e. to chop carrots,
which first offer ideal resistance, then noble surrender.
Slant the blade forward in the initial incision
and, when meeting resistance, bring down the back end
decisively hard to get a resonant thunk on the thick
chopping board, severed segments not fraying or tearing
or clinging, but at once springing cleanly apart to release
a fresh scent. To involve all five senses I chew a firm chunk.

Chuang Tzu tells of King Wen Hui's cook who explained to his king why
he's used only one knife in nineteen years:
'In cutting up oxen, an exceptional cook will chop and need a new knife
every year. An ordinary cook will hack and need a new knife every month.
The mistake is in trying to master the ox. For many years I too attempted to
dominate ... and finally learned not to force but submit.
I surrender to knife, knife surrenders to ox, and then ox surrenders to knife
and to me. So now I don't hack, or even cut, but trust the blade to find a path.
Teach us to control the knife, the other cooks beg, but when I tell them to
surrender they assume it's mockery.'
'Don't you love it?' King Wen Hui laughed. 'The royal advisors talk rubbish
and a butcher explains how to rule.'

Now for the cooking – the process that made us truly human,
transforming not just food but us, by outsourcing much of
the task of digestion, providing more energy for much
less work, thus permitting gut to shrink and brain to grow.
So developed the cooking ape, lord of the flame,
with a smaller belly and bigger brain (though now,

with deep frying, it's back to the other way round).
Cooking fires and communal eating - the beginning
of culture, both of socialisation and solitary musing,
the majority talking (and probably whingeing) but one
apart watching flames leap, crackle, change colour,
glow red and fade out, and thinking finally:
It is all like this, everything flames, flares
and dies into ash that's borne off on the wind.

Cooking is process in search of the unity that leads to emergence,
the new thing more than the sum of the parts, and where pot
and pan may only be stirred, the deep wok may be seized,
lifted, hefted, tossed, swirled. The cook hefting and tossing
and swirling a wok is a God with the crucible of creation
in a strong, right hand. In the fire and the fury
a precarious order on the border with chaos. Flirting
with danger, I toss in a little more chilli and ginger.
Cooking is teaching ... and I am the teacher, my students
the prawns. In they go, sure this is torture but acquiring
spiciness and flavour, in the merging, the union,
becoming themselves, acquiring body and colour.

Then it's the time of knife and fork, no mere utensils
but cautionary examples of the shifting, unpredictable nature
of power. For thousands of years the knife ruled over boards,
a shining sovereign rising in the homage of light, then cutting
and spearing, lord of the feast. But the Renaissance introduced,
along with its glorious masterworks, the equally influential fork,
and a century later Thomas Coryate, first foodie tourist and laureate,
author of *Crudities Hastily Gobbled Up*, brought it to England.
This early fork still had only two tines - but soon got a third,
and in the eighteenth century the efficient Germans put in
the optimal fourth. But what anonymous genius *curved* the tines
to recreate, in the apparently-civilised, Enlightenment hand,
the exhilarating sense of an unsheathed claw? A claw
that poses as refined but combines the two bestial instincts
- stab and grab. This cunning hypocrite soon tamed the table knife,
making it round-bellied, blunting its point and edge and by the end
of the nineteenth century the fork's domination was complete,
as acknowledged in *Social Customs* by Florence Howe Hall:
'The fork is now the favourite and fashionable utensil

for conveying food to the mouth. First it crowded out
the knife, and now the spoon is pretty-well also subdued,
and the fork, insolent and triumphant, is a sumptuary tyrant'.

More edifying is the saintly acceptingness of the plate,
like the halo of Francis, or Mary's immaculate white heart.
And beneath this the table that supports like a parent,
unnoticed, unthanked, though leaned on every day,
often splattered, burned, scratched, but never withdrawing,
collapsing, evading, to be found at all times where and as
it should be, with its feet on the ground but suggesting to all
a higher level of living, a level-headed gathering, sharing,
debating. Our convener of social meals ('getting together
round a table'), and broker of honest deals ('putting your cards
on the table'), the table is the sturdy base of civilisation.
Like Van Heflin in *Shane*, it's unglamorous, foursquare
and plain, always taking the strain, self-effacingly.
Only the weak have to look strong. The true strength,
like goodness, need never be seen. When resentment
invades and overwhelms, I lay hands on this old kitchen table
for strength. Don't complain - take the strain.

And, always assuming the brace position, the humble wooden
kitchen chair spreads wide its legs to take the strain, steadfast
and stalwart, though it sometimes becomes a wind instrument
when it acts as a sounding board for a fart, and gives it sonority,
resonance, volume, like the Elgar cello concerto's prolonged,
dramatic opening note, a resounding, compelling *Hear Ye*!
Rejoice, captive children of doubt and fear,
for the nomad wind knows no constraint.

Rejoice, pilgrims! No Masters, no Doctrine, no Way
and no Grail - and no legendary temple or city awaits,
but the dragons on the path are real and have to be slain.
Whereupon they're reborn and return. The dark ages
are gone but dark urges return ... and will always return ...
the stinginess, resentment, reluctance and rage,
the black heart wanting only the bare attic room,
to commune with spiders, dust and mould,
and cry out in contempt to those below, I want

and need nothing and no one. Fuck off to you all.

As a useful reminder of what I was once but don't wish
to repeat, the fourth portion of fruit is a bowl of the blackberries
I once picked and ate with the toughs in the Lucky Lane,
where blackberries thrived on neglect, dust and dirt,
their mission statement bitter and short: *Never want
to be loved. Stay rebarbative. Harshly subsist, slyly spread
and exult in contrariness.* So bushes thrust berry-hung
branches through fences ... and when eager hands reached
for fruit ripped the soft flesh. Black, maroon, pink and green
on the same bush ... *same branch.* Like the families
of street toughs, with children of every age, and something
of that scornful, family-against-the-world attitude.
Don't fuck with us. We're the blackberries.
The fruit self-destructed on touch. Not a berry at all,
an assembly of ink-filled exploding spheres ... cluster bomb,
though when it detonated inside the mouth a tart shock wave
aroused tired synapses to flash: *Life is good but not sweet.*
No wonder mother despised them and served only mandarin oranges,
peeled, stoned, segmented and tinned in thick syrup. It would
reaffirm her view of me as an idiot if she learned that I actually *paid*
for these. *What? Two pounds fifty ... for those old things ...*

The quest hero comes home, but not to sneer, nor, as in quest sagas,
bring enlightenment to his people. At his first attempt to stray
from their perpetual facetiousness he'd be run out of town
for presumption. *Who does he think he is? Thinks he is somebody.*
He has come back to look, to see again the town with his old
but new eyes, from the railway station emerging into a splendour
of light on water. And in these small towns no one walks any more
so he has to himself a majestic bridge over a river as wide as the Thames.
'Who looks upon a river in a meditative hour and does not recall
the flux of all things?' wondered Emerson. 'Throw a stone into the stream,
and the circles that propagate themselves are the beautiful type
of all influence.' Ahead is the town and behind is the hill of Corrody,
home of the mover who groaned, roared and swore as he hauled
through the city apartment the furniture sent by the quest hero's mother
(still loath to accept that the quest requires only a staff and a bowl),
breaking a leg of the sofa and ripping the back of a chair
of the quality, three-piece suite, before slumping down with a last oath

to look around sceptically: 'Much did this cost ye?' When told:
'Fuck Ah bought a wee house in Corrody for five hundred poun'.'
Despising the city, and proud of his bluntness in the devious
metropolis, (though of course he would boil with fury if the city
scorned the town). But soon silent as God to the mother's enraged
compensation demands, an unmoved mover remote and on high.
And here are the quays, no longer the rotting wood piles
where he came as a boy with the street toughs for mystery and danger.
Why was a rough-looking middle-aged woman in a white sheath dress
and white high-heeled shoes toiling up the narrow gangway
of a rusty old tub? Now the quayside is landscaped, with trees and shrubs,
even a sculpture commemorating victims – an upside-down
bronze woman, cruelly bomb-flung. Compassion and art – the old
cynical nihilism must be no more. But a closer approach shows a scrawl
of indelible black on her crotch: *Sniff Me Hole*. He is home.

He is back not to criticise but to look … and to listen.
Mother is dying – and surely now will talk about her disappointing life?
Surely at last they will be reconciled? Surely she can not still
resent *his* life? And indeed she is mild, meditative, surprised at his ability
to keep house and cook, and grateful for this. Wanting indeed
to talk, or so it seems, but able only to discuss the banal.
This is what happens in petrifaction, the change brought about
by resistance to change. Those who refuse to talk seriously
lose the ability to talk. When the time comes to speak their jaws
lock and tongues freeze. The hearts yearn and ache
but the mouths cannot speak. Nor can *he* express thanks
for the love of a mother, that selfless attention that every child
needs but few get. Always her son, he can never voice gratitude
for the lifelong security of the loved child and stable beginning,
albeit heavily circumscribed. Even standing on the shoulders
of dwarfs gets us nearer the stars. And so they take refuge
in banality once more. 'Will you take some old rubbish
to the dump for me?' 'Of course. Where's the dump?'
But her old peevishness and impatience resurface.
'*Everyone* knows where the dump is.' 'No. *I* don't know where it is.
I haven't lived here in decades. There was no dump in my time.
Municipal dumps didn't even *exist*.' But nothing enrages her more
than such calm, irrefutable statement of fact, the very height
of cunning smartaleckry. And to use a word like *municipal*.
She attempts to control herself – but all of her lifelong resentment
bursts out in a wild scream, vindicating once more

her practical wisdom and rejecting his infantile idiocy:
'EVERYONE KNOWS WHERE THE DUMP IS.'

And grievous the news from the USA - the baseball-capped,
check-shirted Master is dead. Everyone (and everything) dies,
the most simple and obvious fact of the world but always
the hardest to comprehend. The Master seemed
on a tranquil plateau - but there is only descent.
We are not meant to abide but to take the long slide.

And Jimmy dead. Stewart dead. Bray too, defence
of the Nietzschean nihilists. Even Boyle the boyish striker.
Bray, rock in every emergency, ash in an urn in Wimbledon.
Boyle, the life of every party, bones in cold wet Irish earth.

My cynical townspeople, here is the joke of it:
I am trying *not* to be somebody. The lessons of insignificance
are deep but difficult to take to heart. So the Goddess,
profoundly compassionate, has revealed our insignificance
only bit by shocking bit. No, you are not the hub of the whole thing
but a grain of dust on a chunk of rock that's a minor satellite
of a minor star that is one among billions on the fringe of a galaxy
that is one among billions, and even your universe may not be unique,
merely one among yet another multitude, you increasingly
infinitesimal speck, who are not God's elect but 98% ape
and 90% mouse and even more than 50% of the fruit fly,
your supposedly immortal soul and worldly self
transient illusions, in the rushing flow vortices
of turbulence that appear to be stable, immutable essences.
So the self's major feat is convincing itself it exists.
Hence the human core competence - self deceit.

Then Yeh Chueh says: 'I was given an urgent message to deliver but
somewhere along the way I lost the address.

For a long time this troubled me - until one day I unsealed the message …
and found an entirely blank scroll.'

'There *is* no message and no address,' the Master explains. 'Hence the need
for zealous messengers has never been more great.'

'I can't follow you, Master.'

'Therefore you are finally fit to be a follower. Leave me to walk with me.'
'But where is the path?'
'It is not the path that makes the walk but the walk that makes the path.'
'And where will *you* walk, Master?'
'Into the unknown.'
'Where bandits roam?'
'Dead drunk, I rolled down the mountain path. Sober, I would have broken bones.'
'But in which direction lies the unknown?'
'To venture into the unknown go where all have gone before.'

To be wary of logic but never irrational.
To reject truth as absolute but not think it relative.
To find no foundation for values and yet espouse values.
To abhor righteous certainty and yet believe strongly.
To acknowledge change but not worship novelty.
To accept without becoming resigned.
To define without becoming defined.
To venerate matter but not be a materialist.
To cherish ideas but not be an ideologue.
To be agog at mystery but not be a mystagogue.
To love work but focus on process not goal.
To love learning, the verb, but hate the noun.
To accept bottom-up but not reject top-down.
To immerse in depths but not drown.
To transcend while keeping both feet on the ground.
To remain detached but not remote.
To expose the absurd but not to hurt.
To have tensions but not be pulled apart.
To suspect we're fucked but still hope.

And maybe it never gets better or worse, but just changes.
Maybe it is never easier or harder, just different.
Every answer generating a host of new questions.
Every solution a new kind of problem. Every gain also a loss.

Freedom! The modern world cried at the tyrant gods,
only let all be free and all shall be well.
But the ecstasy of freedom leads to the agony of choice,
the dream of the infinite to the closure of finitude,

and the promise of liberation to the crushing new burden
of having to work it all out from first principles
when there are no first principles. At least it's
a wee change, as mother would say. Once we suffocated
under constraint. Now we drown in an ocean of choice.

Illusions, illusions. We know that the Wizard was exposed
as a fraud. And now we learn that Jack Palance was no good
on a horse. In the scene where he first encounters Shane
– tense but wordless, those who know do not speak –
he has to remount with lithe ease, which he clumsily failed
to achieve. Cool, sinister grace, Jack, *for Christ's sake*.
But no. So they simply replayed his *dis*mounting backways.
'You can't break the mould,' Shane eventually tells the boy.
But where is this factory of rigid moulds? No mould but time
and the clay itself, soft and wet, squeezed and stretched,
punctured and pummelled, rounded and flattened by what happens
to happen – the revelatory aleatory, the plastic stochastic.
'Fantastic!' I cry now, released from my fate as an arid despiser
to venture down into the fecund world, immerse in the tumult of
contingency and the tangle of connexity, the squalor of democracy
and the tension of marriage: 'I will live with one woman,
love the myriad creatures and fruits of the earth
and attend to and cherish the ten thousand things.'

'If you cannot be free of yourself,' asks Lao Tzu,
'how will you ever become yourself?' The fully-realised self
knows it's not even there. So take your self to the mirror
and lecture it: *Listen, big shot, you don't even exist.*

Then the cunning self answers, 'Of course I'm illusory,
you perceptive observer. But just try to change me.'
Whereupon the two laugh together. For this is the fate
of self-awareness – laughing into a dark mirror.

The manifest world, the Sufis said, was created as a gallery
of mirrors designed to reflect the glory of God.
Thus it is necessary to look in a mirror, not to learn
to be a self that projects, but a mirror that reflects.

'Therefore cut yourself off from yourself,'
counselled Ayn al-Qozāt Hamadāni 'that the sun
of grace may shine according to the polish of your soul.'

'To find the true self,' also added the Master, 'is to learn there's no self. To find
the true Way is to see there's no path.

And to find the true faith is to know there's no truth. In whatever direction
the seeking, nothing awaits, nothing is there.

Nothing is always our destination. Nothing is what we must understand.
Nothing is what we must learn to know.'

Yeh Chueh stops and plants his staff on the earth. 'This means there's no
purpose in journeys, no purpose in study.'

'On the contrary, it means there is everything to seek and learn. For only
those who know everything can know they know nothing.'

The universe, physicists tell us now, developed from a quantum
fluctuation in a vacuum. So the whole thing emerged
out of nothing, which is volatile and fecund.
Even the void is a self-starter. Even nothing has to become.
And I will soon become nothing so I must ponder
nothing. I will stop at nothing to understand,
and I will connect nothing with nothing, link the nothing
of the West to the nothing of the East. Now over all the earth
nothing rules. Therefore never be deceived by a solid
appearance. Go in more deeply. There's nothing to it.

If we have peeled the onion to its empty core, are we left
with only tears in our eyes? Yes indeed - but tears of mirth.
When nothingness jumped out to shout *Boo!* I laughed till
I cried. And in fact the supreme laugh is laughing at nothing.
To laugh at nothing is to laugh at everything,
with a mirth that starts deep in the body as a seizure
that makes the innards quake, then the torso vibrate,
like a tuning fork in time with the laughter of God,
before mounting to squeeze tight the face and force tears
through the eyes. This laughter's a physical mover and shaker,
counteracting petrifaction with convulsion, and sclerosis
with flow, and laughter at nothing has the extra advantage
of infuriating everyone even more than laughter at something.
'What are you laughing at *now*?' mother snapped.

'Nothing,' I gasped, in an even wilder paroxysm.

So appreciate the magnificence
Of complete insignificance,

The underground festival
Of the infinitesimal,

The clandestine rule
Of the minuscule.

Lie low and flourish
Or chest beat and perish.

Failure is hurtful
But triumph is fatal.

As the tiny know, co co co
Is the way to go go go.

Coevolve and contrive,
Codepend and connive.

Remember the low life whence we came. We come not
just from apes but from slime. We are not aristocrats
but the scum of the earth. We are not the chosen ones
but merely animated water, walking mineral assemblages,
bags of bugs, communities of immigrants, and immigrants
with the qualities prized by a host, cooperative, diligent
and nearly invisible, capable of surviving inhospitable environments
and willing to do the dirty jobs. We depend on our microbes,
as they do on us, especially the multitude of symbionts in our guts,
crowded main home of the microbiome in the Democratic
People's Republic of Me. So when I speak with reverence
of my inner life I don't mean my soul but the bugs in my gut.
More bugs in the stomach than stars in the galaxy
(Walt was right to claim that he contained multitudes).
The human body is a planet more variously populated even
than earth, and with many more continents whose tribes rarely meet,
so the armpit people never know the assholes, nor the teeming
population of the gut the distant tribes between the toes.
(Though thanks to modern forms of communication the mouth

and the genital peoples have got to know each other well.)
And I salute the other invisible workers, the bacteria
who have helped make my favourite things, coffee,
bread, cheese and wine, and who hang out in some of
my favourite places - the beloved's mouth, vagina and anus.

I acknowledge my debt to the microbiome … and, since
these little guys really know symbiosis (they invented it),
they reward with the gift of a late evening motion, unexpected
and startling, without even the littlest premonitory fartlet,
and not an oriental but an *American-sized* portion
that flows like the River of Heraclitus, who is said to have died
by drowning, which would surely have been appropriate
- except that it was not in his river but in liquid cowshit.
God likes to give things an educational twist.
Bright, insouciant beginnings, ignominious ends.
William Holden, dead drunk, falling down stairs dead.
Or Elvis dying on a toilet seat. I hope
he left the building on a surge strong as mine.

In fact mutualism is not a response to, but precedes,
competition and is the foundational fact of life.
The cell is a symbiotic union with the mitochondrion,
a hostile, invading bacterium. The smart cell, as crafty
as capitalism, said to itself, Let's *incorporate* the little fucker,
make it worth his while to make use of the organism, which will
then make use of *him*. And eventually the mitochondrion
became institutionalised and could no longer survive on its own.
Nor could the cell survive without the mitochondrion.
Nor would we, nor any of the creatures of earth, exist,
nor could any survive, without this basic union at the heart
of complex life. Yet the union is never serene but continual
tension, a tug of war. Tension is energy. Tension is life.

Always the complementarity of polarity. Tension in matter
(electron and proton), tension in nature (male and female),
tension in organisation (bottom-up and top-down),
and tension in bodies (heart and head). So my heart says
go left and my head says go right, my heart says look up
and my head says looks down, my heart says *go in*

and my head says *get out*, my head calls for justice
and my heart begs for mercy, my head says *climb up to
high windows* and my heart says *for Christ's sake come down*.
And tension even within the head, the left brain literal,
linear, practical, totally humourless and frequently angry
(the only emotion it knows), and the right brain imaginative,
associative, humorous, totally unpractical (and experiencing
every emotion but anger). The left brain top-down, the right brain
bottom-up, the left keen to dominate and the right keen to ruminate,
left keen to order, and right to discover. 'If you could just
leave off daydreaming *for a minute*,' snaps the left brain,
'I will outline for you the five-year plan.' Whereupon the right brain
shakes with laughter … and the left shakes with fury. But when
shaking subsides they combine in harmonious tension, fruitful strife.

Tension's the universal animator – of atom, cell, democracy
and marriage, the crack of the spark between opposite charges,
the thrum of the rope in the tug of war. But no tension in Heaven,
so God is morose, missing Lucifer, who could give him
an argument, and even more importantly, make him laugh.

No resolution of tension. I'm a positive nihilist, a mystical scientist,
a sensual rationalist, an empathising sociopath and a long-married eremite,
the man in the tower and the man in the crowd, sometimes a solitary,
sometimes a symbiont, sometimes a paragon, sometimes a cunt,
and beginning now to enjoy the chaotic serenity, anarchic discipline
and voluptuous austerity of age. Living is largely tension management,
the establishing and maintenance of energising tensions.
Grasp the powerful contradictions, pulling ferociously
in opposite directions, and hold them together for bracing strength.

       My lack of faith will save my soul.
       My crazy heart will keep me sane.
       My shattered hopes will make me whole.
       My broken back will take the strain.

       The prison of age will set me free.
       The heedless world will make me care.
       The meaninglessness will be the key.
       The grinning void will hear my prayer.

Let paradox resign to rule
As I control by letting go,
Grow again by feeling small,
Learn in order not to know.

And the final quest hero tale of seeking the grail offers no grail,
no tale and no hero ... not even a quest. Vladimir and Estragon
just wait for Godot. Cowardly and lazy? Or possibly braver
than journeys and trials their noble, heroic, endless waiting?
But a country road is cold and bleak so they decide to wait
at home for Godot to phone or email, text or tweet, link in to
a social network site or appear on some one of the three hundred
channels they check in turn with the remote. Instead comes
a traditional knock on the door. What greater fear than to get
what you've waited for? The pair are transfixed by sheer terror.
A second knock - louder and angrier. Estragon, shivering,
parts curtains: 'Dressed all in black ... with a black helmet
hiding his face. Is it Godot ... or Death? *Or is Godot Death?*'
Vladimir picks up the fallen remote. 'Just our pizzas, you fool.'

Always Vladimir and Estragon will continue to wait.
We are not required to complete the quest - but neither, it seems,
are we free to desist. 'This thing whereof we all speak,
it can never be found by our seeking,' noted Abu Yasid al-Bistami,
'yet only the seeker can find it.' So let the illusion take our hands
and lead us up the garden path and let the horizon throb with allure
behind the cloud of dust that laughs, as *Homo absurdus*
admits that no grail can exist, and then goes forth
in search of it anyway, walking in trainers enhanced by
Masai Barefoot Technology, with a state-of-the-art staff
(the Trekrite anti-shock aluminium walking pole with folding stool),
and an ultra-lightweight Superdry backpack with external MP3
player compartment and all-round zip access for the tupperware
container of (pole-and-line-caught) tuna salad, Braeburn apples,
sparkling water, wet wipes, Mosiguard and Afterbite.

Among the major twentieth-century discoveries, with quantum
mechanics, chaos theory, the middle manager and spray-on cheese:
that *Homo sapiens* is fundamentally absurd, the ape that has

learned it is only an ape and therefore can never behave like an ape,
the self that has learned there is no self but strives desperately
to be true to itself, and the seeker for meaning who's learned
there's no meaning but is always obliged to continue the seeking.

So make noise for *Homo absurdus* – the ape that can walk
and cook, talk and joke, read and write, think and seek,
and connect things to other things, the maker of analogies.
Thoreau: 'All perception of truth is the detection of analogy'.

If we can't find a new, reconfigure the old, rummage in
and ransack the Ten Thousand Things. Appropriate,
associate, relate and curate. It's the time of the hybrids,
amalgams and blends, of mongrel breeders,
patchwork weavers, collage artists, fusion chefs.
Our core competence is to copy and paste.
The best sampling and mixing machine is the brain.

The lesson of nature, that genius junk sculptor:
it is not the ingredients but the way they're combined.
Humans may have many fewer genes than bananas
but ingenious permutation helps us outperform the fruit.

Connection! Connection! The name is McMenamin.
A victory over the tyranny of time! *Danny* McMenamin
… better still. *Ah* … there they all are. Night is falling
on the street and lights are coming on in houses,
though not in McCrossan's living room, radiant only
with divine luminescence. Huddled round the window
in the concrete front garden, in reverent silence
the faithful worship, still, rapt and wan in God's
flickering glow, as, dripping shit, howling in shame
and rage, Danny McMenamin runs down the dim street.

I have kept to last my favourite, the apricot, most forthright
of fruits, lacking front, the same all the way through,
skin and flesh the same hue, therefore perfect, beloved,
for you – lioness-tawny-warm and nape-of-neck downy soft,

with a cleft hinting subtly at *cul* and that optimal balance
of firmness and yield. Go on ... *squeeze*. It won't squash
or squirt into your face, but ungrudgingly open to show
a stone, startlingly dark and detached, that won't cling
to the flesh (as it does in the plum). At the heart
of the sensuous - probity, rectitude, but no Northern
apple's marmoreal hauteur (*my* ancestors posed for Chardin
and Cézanne), fulvous halves like the rounded roof tiles
of Provence when love's shutters flung wide onto late afternoon
and the low late sun aurified abdomen, heavy breasts,
rich double cream of the spread inner thighs, made glitter
the studs in the gusset - three coins in a fountain -
and made shine, like spring's early snowdrops,
the white toilet-tissue flecks dotting the secret lips
... so that my own lips scarcely could open because my heart
was in my mouth. Wild the cherishing heart in the perishing flesh.
Lord, suffer my cry to come unto thee and in her furrow
my tongue shall announce thy praise. I would gladly leave
life in the conjoining of love, in an ultimate unity of process
come and go at the same time. The Goddess sprawled over those
sheets in the sun like a great tawny lioness after a kill and feed.
Now a tremor of ecstasy remembered traverses me.
I'm tenderly, sweetly, exquisitely stiff. But I will
save every drop of my impetuous ejaculate.
I will not touch my lad. I will not pull my plum.

But instead clean the home. I will banish my old friend
the dust (temporarily at least), have the floor and the furniture
gleaming in light softly dimmed, in the Chinese vase fresh
wild flowers blooming (but my wild nostril hair freshly trimmed).
I will put out the rubbish and put in a sparkling wine,
plump up the throw cushions, turn down the lights.

The beloved returns. She returns. To offer once again my eyes,
my arm, my twisted grin, to say once more those sovereign words:
Let's walk together through the streets and note the qualities
of people. Come, my queen. Then, later, forth together
by the sun-burnished sea of the legendary lovers - Cleopatra
and Anthony, Helen and Paris, Medea and Jason. I beg
the new Oracle: Search Engine, find somewhere warm that will
ease weary body and soul. 'No problem,' answers the Oracle,

'why not a monk's cell (with double bed) in a monastery
in the mountains, close to God but closer still to the Med?'

We could honour the cell, and the origin of life, by recreating
symbiotic union in a cell. But what of the quest for the perfect meal?
We can't evolve backwards to eat in a *canteen*? No, the monastery
has *four* restaurants, and a shop which seems … this website photo
is so small, unfocused … but yes, yes … appears to sell wine.

Then in cool pristine mornings long walks in the hills.
No, walking's not enough. Walking is merely the body's prose.
Women love the body's poetry of dance. Search Engine,
seek out a salsa class and enrol us at once. I should have danced
more with my beloved, when the heart was hearty and the limbs
were limber, when the brain and the body were brighter, quicker,
but time and the world were slower, richer, and the nights
were occult and eternal, the dance floor enchanted
and fragrantly carnal, under the glitterball and under the moon.

From the outer galaxies to the heart of the atom,
everything dances, both planets and particles moving in sync,
as do the cells in living things. For the whole thing began
with a dance. In the night of Brahman nature was still.
But Shiva, the Great Lord, rose up in his rapture,
entwined with a serpent and aureoled with fire,
yet with countenance serene, and danced the rudra tandava,
which sent waves through all inert matter. Then, behold,
matter also began to dance, becoming in its energy
and radiance the manifestation of Shiva's glory.
Hence the atoms' jitterbug and the galaxies' stately minuet,
the dance of the cells and the dance of thought.

    Dance because all things are always on fire.
        Dance because everything flows.
    Dance, for whatever your heart's desire,
        Downstream in flames it all goes.

    Dance because dance is the process incarnate,
        Constantly changing but always one.

Dance like the leaves of the tree trapped in concrete.
    Dance like the house dust in sun.

Dance like the neurons that vibrate together.
    Dance like the heart and the blood.
Dance like the quarks at the heart of all matter.
    Dance like the stars and the void.

Dance because dance knows that nothing's for ever,
    Dance understands it's all go.
Dance because dance is the flame and the river,
    Dance is the fire become flow.

Come, take my cold hand, lead me back down from the chilly
high window and out to the sweaty dance floor. Every living thing
has rhythm. Rhythm beats in every cell and every organ
has a rhythm section laying down a beat, from the pacemaker beat
of the heart to the pulsating rings of the gut and the waves
that surge in time across the illuminated brain. As Duke explained,
also in rhythm, *It don't mean a thing if it aint got that swing.*

My circadian rhythm section always keeps time - in the morning
a jubilant drum roll and cymbal crash, at evening the brushes'
soft circular swish. At first light the dance is a wild jitterbug,
and at twilight a slow, shuffling cheek to cheek hug.
Dawn resolves and dusk absolves, the compassionate
mother who sighs: 'Again nothing accomplished?
Never mind. Hush now, my wayward child.'

Evening escapes from the lords of the absolute, tyrants of day,
who claim, as though by divine right, to separate, control, direct.
Now the mind and the world may associate freely, at one in the flow,
the enchanting succession without distinction of fading light.

Dawn and dusk, the times of transition, are the times of inspiration.
Who thinks of anything new in the somnolent, sluggish afternoon?
Dawn and dusk, when the birds sing, in transports of transit,
their paeans of change at the waxing and waning,
the shining and fading, the waking and sleeping ...

at dawn in jubilation and at dusk in gratitude.

Softly at evening, softly sing, in surfeit, gratitude and tenderness.
The full day wanes, the strong light fades.
A rustle, a fragrance, a breath, a caress.
Now already with thee, Goddess. Tender is the almost night.

Evening murmurs once more of the uncontrollable,
uncontainable, unrepeatableness of the world,
the beautiful wanton never beholden, making a mockery
of all who would hold her. The whole thing refuses analysis,
breaks the laws, laughs at the forecasts, pees on the dogmas,
smirks at the paradigms, hoodwinks the algorithms
and escapes through an acausal hole in spacetime.

The product of process is process. The answers to questions
are questions. The prize for the quest is another quest.
At the heart of the complexity – ambiguity.
At the heart of the knowledge – ignorance.
At the heart of the stone and the steel – Shiva's dance.
Therefore let the eyes glitter with strange revelation,
face twist in what might be a sort of a grin, for time is
the wave with no clue where it's going but mad to get there,
and change is the churn with no clue what it's making
but mad to discover, while every puny, blind, deluded self
believes it understands, is in control and choreographs
the dance of chance. So the world is a Festival of
Naked Emperors and life is absurd ... but *divinely* absurd.

Then be not disturbed by illusions of isolation, repetition,
monotony or servitude. For where is the state that is static,
the thing that will never connect or react, the events
that exactly repeat or the absolute truth to dictate?
Nor be disturbed by the cravings. True freedom is not
being free to have whatever you want but being free
from the compulsion to have what you want.
Prithee, nuncle, be content. Let your heavy heart
be buoyant and your tread on earth be light.

As God became man to redeem humankind, now infinity
and eternity assume space and time. They want us to repent,
reject the heresy of self … merge again with the whole thing
… belong … reunite. There is unity under the fragmentation,
homeliness at the heart of the alienation, a simplicity beyond
the complexity, a naivety and innocence beyond knowingness.

So much briefly, strangely, flaring. I can be written off
but not written out. Mortality's a deathless theme.
Again the rhapsode rises up in my old pipsqueak carcase and sings.
Again the measure moves my costive heart and laggard limbs.
Flow, Heraclitus River, till I end my song and dance.
Melodeon of the universe, play your jig, expanding, contracting
and bouncing back, as the galaxies accelerate away, breeding stars
that are born, burn and die in supernova explosions
or collapse into black holes that sing, dance, explode and collide
to send tsunamis through spacetime, while Saturn rains
diamonds, WASP 12B rains rubies, 55canceriE rains rock,
Miranda, the moon of Uranus, more like an old rock group
than an old rock, constantly breaks up and reforms,
and, here below, the River of Heraclitus flows into the ocean
of Leibniz, which makes the wave of William James,
which blindly sweeps us on, and is ever taller, stronger, wilder.
Go along with it and swim – or go against, struggle … drown.
Four things no use to those at sea, Machado warned us
– anchor, rudder, oars … and the fear of going down.

Another twilight insight – Alan Ladd was wrong as Shane
… too dainty, too pretty. Those ridiculous buckskins.
That neatly combed hair. It should have been someone
with dangerous charm, rougher, stronger, more louche
… Glenn Ford as he was in *The 3.10 to Yuma.*
Surely the director's first choice was Glenn Ford?
Search Engine, Oracle, Omniscient One, tell me
the insight of twilight was right. No, the first choice
was Montgomery Clift. Who would also have been wrong
in a different way … too anguished, too sensitive.
Once more I weep for the doomed quest hero,
the lovely, yearning older woman and the worshipful boy
whose heart is broken. Recalling my increasingly sensitive skin,

I have this final thought on quest heroes like Shane, riding on in
the pitiless dust and sun: How did they cope without moisturising
cream … and what state must their groins have been in?

No quest in the sun for the ageing quest hero. No action.
No movement. No trials. No talk. Silence. Night.
An old house. Motionless in strong light,
a white head beneath a black Anglepoise lamp.

The black lamp with its bent back and head
is a cowled monk at work in a scriptorium,
illuminating a manuscript, while the books behind,
rising up, shelf upon shelf, are a colloquy of hierophants
in the gallery of heaven, and religiously black
the austere Penguin Classics, now almost as old
as their owner, and increasingly like him,
frayed, deeply lined, yellowing, growing dark
liver spots, brittle, frail - ready to fall apart.

I take down *The Winged Energy of Delight*,
let it fall open randomly and inhale its scent deeply.
These spread white pages are indeed angel wings,
strong enough to lift up the heaviest heart.
And sometimes, as hungry for plunder as Alexander,
I ransack and loot. In callow youth I stole the books.
In cunning age I steal the words. Reading is deviant
… *criminal* … identity theft. Gloatingly I caress
my wooden shelves, so rarely appreciated like every support,
(e.g. those invisible quadrupeds, table, chair, bed),
the wood roughly-sawed and unplaned to remind me
to honour the unvarnished truth. So I rasp my thumb
on a splintery edge to experience afresh the rough weave
of the world, and agree that we may be here only to say, but say
properly, bowl and book, pencil, shelf, nostril-hair trimmer.

… And corkscrew, the one with the slim, Audrey Hepburn arms
and hieratic Henry Moore head, an upper half that only becomes
a full body when decisively united with a bottle of wine.
Then the head slowly turns as the slender arms rise up

in jubilant homage to Dionysus, dancer God of the grape,
and the palms open, ask to be taken and gently drawn down
so the cork rises up in the breast like a buoyant heart.
Evensong - the soft resonant pop and the sweet
goo-goo-goo ... a-guh-guh of poured wine.

On the consolations of wine the despisers and affirmers
are finally one. 'Be always drunken, only this matters,'
raved Baudelaire. 'For any sort of aesthetic activity
or perception,' claimed Nietzsche, a fervent disciple
of Dionysus, 'the essential state is intoxication.'
'Not with intellect alone,' agreed even the Sage
of Concord, Emerson, 'but with the intellect inebriated
by nectar'. For William James wine was an entry-level
mystical experience: 'Sobriety diminishes, discriminates,
and says no; drunkenness expands, unites, and says yes.'
'On wide roads of wonder,' sang Hafiz,
'wine leads the mind forth. Come, Saqi, more wine,
that I may pass on my news of the mystery.'

Complicitous wine and compassionate night.
Secret hour of the tryst, lovers silent and still,
too enraptured to speak. The roles fade,
the masks drop, the lines blur, the veils part.
Softly the soul and the cosmos consort.

Equal in splendour the shining and dimming.
Equal in strangeness the burning and yearning.
Not aggressive but caressive is the soft evening wind.
Something rustles. Something creaks. *O come in,*
equivocator. Nothing is clear or distinct, as everything
mingles beyond isolation, beyond distillation.
Awe and ache are one in the sigh of the night.
But never the bitterness of regret, only the tenderness of rue.
That love and praising came so late. And that it is over so soon,
with so many good already gone, incredulous, into the night
(and incredulous also those who remain). For having thought
so little of so much (contemptuous and dismissive in the emporium
of marvels), while persistently thinking so much of so little
(the superior, knowing, unique individual), gravity's revenge

brings vaulting arrogance to earth. First down to earth,
and then under the earth, which will keep no respectful distance
but worm its way into the sovereign heart. The grave is not
eternal peace but a lively new meet and greet. That the guest at
the feast will become the feast is the shocking price of the free meal.
All that feeds becomes feed, and the price for the consciousness
of the outrageous novelty of being alive is the consciousness
of the even more outrageous novelty of having to die.

    All change here, please! All change!
    Forget reassuring geriatric repose.
    For time speeds up as the body slows,
        The rejected becomes the ideal
            The banal the surreal
    The familiar the surpassingly strange.

    Moving less easily but more easily moved,
    There are often now mystified tears
    Instead of youth's rational sneers,
        The late blessing of wonder
            Spiked with terror,
    Nothing even understood much less proved.

    First a swelled head, then swelled feet.
    The jubilant worms are saying grace,
    Not even earth a resting place
        For the head that earns,
          The heart that yearns,
    The immortal soul that's condemned meat.

Out with my glass to the yard to enhance my insignificance.
The Goddess has steadily shrunk us so that the universe may expand.
Humility and nullity are the portals of wonder. You have to
think small to think big, shrink close to nothing to squeeze through
and pass beyond. Recall that the universe grew from a point,
the earth from a grain of dust, life from a single cell.
Treasure the minuscule. Honour the small. Now I understand
my minuscule meaningless role in the majestical meaninglessness
of the whole - the squeak of a twitch in the teeming void.

A clear night, just a few scattered stars high above
the dark bulk of the community centre. I have never known
the names of stars, any more than the names of weeds and bugs.
Too far and too near. Too remote and too familiar.
We do not look at much and the gaze is not prolonged or rich.
We just want to stay at home, protected and entertained.
The satellite dishes look up, the security cameras look down.

At least I know stars do not shine for ever but go through
seven ages like us, on a hectic trajectory from dust to dust.
A star is not cold but a furnace, not still and idle
but busy and practical (baking the elements needed for life),
not eternal but mortal, not individual but part of a galaxy,
dying in explosions of gas and dust, from which form
the clouds that condense into new stars. The dust is a shield
against heat to permit the molecular clouds to cool, protective
dust – and in the birth of the star is a catalyst, nurturing dust.

At least I understand the moon, a po-faced old charlatan,
bleak rock pretending to burn and shine, stealing its light from the sun
to appear mysterious and grand, to pose as the Goddess herself,
if you please, while cleverly locking its spin to our orbit
so we never see its dark side. Aren't we all as two-faced
as the duplicitous moon, always hiding the dark and pretending
to beam like beneficent suns? Well, shine on, or pretend to shine,
you old fraud. You are still an inspiration … of sorts …
If no illumination comes from within, steal a light from without.

And the cosmos itself has a po face, appearing silent, still,
sedate, a remote aged master, when it's more the hyperactive child,
ceaselessly writhing, twisting, fizzing, popping, colliding, exploding,
creating, destroying, dancing, singing. Galaxies dance, albeit slowly,
rotating every few hundred million years – and black holes dance
and sing, albeit down low, with the deepest note known
(deeper even than Leonard Cohen), a deep song in B-flat,
57 octaves below middle C, a million billion times below
the lowest heard by human ears. Like matter that only seems inert,
the cosmos only seems sedate. Both offer a sober demeanour
but are mental in secret, putting to shame their vain creature
who loves to look lively, talk and act, but is secretly inert

and sedate, tame at heart. If the cosmos is old and mad
I should be too … a geriatric ecstatic. The old stars
burn ever more brilliantly … for a time …
with the more intense glow of collapsing fire.

Just about enough time to get my own back on time
With a late efflorescence, a senescent sublime.

So open all the vents and let the dying embers flare.
Let the fleeting final sparks take to the air.

I want to burn. I want to shine. I want to fly. I want to flow.
I want to feel. I want to hear. I want to see. I want to know.

Youth with its keen eyes is blind – but the failing eyes of age
see the burgeoning world. As we go grey the world acquires colour,
as we wither to husks the world blooms with rich growth.
As the limbs no longer limber realise the need to dance,
as the brain becoming dimmer learns it's meant to understand.
We commence knowing nothing and we end knowing nothing
– but the final ignorance is so much richer than the first.
No extending the lease of the merciless dust.
This landlord works only to contract. Yet we must
praise thee, implacable dust. Should I be food for my friends
the worms … or cut out the middle men and go straight to dust?

Endlessly embarking on journeys and trials, the eternal quest
        For the Golden Fleece, The Holy Grail,
        Oz, Godot, dark matter, white whale,
        The Castle, The Master, The Magic Ring,
        A Grand Unified Theory of Everything,
The elixir of immortality or the balmy islands of the blessed,

Children of quantum nothingness and the demiurge of time,
        No more than the flare of a match in wind,
        A momentary flicker in the universal mind
        But driven to search for what doesn't exist,
        The mirage of an answer raised by the dust,
Make your dusty quest a questival, your absurd a sublime.

We ought to be thankful, spoiled for choice to the bitter end,
with a dazzling profusion and variety of dooms.
A pandemic of necrotizing bacterial flesh eaters,
haemorrhage fevers, contagious cancer, airborne AIDS,
or a drug-resistant bubonic plague. A supervolcano eruption
that shoots ash and gas over fifty kilometres high,
where the stratosphere carries it round the globe
to fall in a winter of grey snow. The jellification of oceans,
when the madly proliferating jellyfish link arm in arm
and make the seven seas a single vast gob of snot.
Or the oceans rebel at their appalling mistreatment
and poison the poisonous world with a hydrogen sulphide
burp or a monstrous methane fart. Or the planet is consumed
by the creations of physics - disappearing down into
micro black holes, turned into strange matter by strangelets,
or into a grey ball of nanosludge by replicating nanobots.
Frozen to death by a new ice age or fried by a mad superflare
of the sun, vaporised by a blast from a cosmic ray gun
when a psychopathic type 1c death star explodes.
Or our Milky Way collides with the Andromeda galaxy,
like the thousands of Russian tanks driving head on
into thousands of Tigers in the battle of Kursk.
Or when neutron stars headbutt with mutually fatal force.
Or after a sibling-rival clash between Sirius A and Sirius B
(B was once bigger but is now a white dwarf and may seek revenge).
Or when God, despite attending an anger management class,
hurls a meteor at the earth in a new fit of wrath.
Or, in the ultimate vandalism, the dark energy goes ape
and tears the universe apart in The Big Rip.

And if the planet survives long enough the sun will become
a red giant and die, although not before returning the planet
to dust, the all-singing-dancing-and-laughing dust,
unto which I too return soon. But grieve not, my golden queen.
It seems to end … but never ends. We'll be reborn. Our dusts
will seek each other out and dance among the mortal stars.
Though probably none of this tonight. There's probably time
for another glass to toast the whole thing once again.

The whole thing is to praise the whole thing, forge a fulsome
encomium to the harmony of antinomy, the plenitude

of finitude, the surge of the demiurge, the flex of the flux,
the complexity of the connexity, the ebriety of variety,
the afflatus of chaos, the dance of chance.
To be a tingling sensorium in the teeming emporium
– a unity of unities, a process of processes!
Who could be self-important? Who could be sensible?
Who could be logical? I'm crazy about the whole thing.